FROM SENTENCES TO ESSAYS

A Guide to Reflective Writing through Reflective Thinking
Student's Edition

Mara Cogni
Oslo Adult Education Center Sinsen, Norway

Series in Education

Copyright © 2019 Vernon Press, an imprint of Vernon Art and Science Inc, on behalf of the author.

All rights reserved. No part of this publication may be reproduced, stored in a retrieval system, or transmitted in any form or by any means, electronic, mechanical, photocopying, recording, or otherwise, without the prior permission of Vernon Art and Science Inc.

www.vernonpress.com

In the Americas:	In the rest of the world:
Vernon Press	Vernon Press
1000 N West Street,	C/Sancti Espiritu 17,
Suite 1200, Wilmington,	Malaga, 29006
Delaware 19801	Spain
United States	

Series in Education
Library of Congress Control Number: 2018947520
ISBN: 978-1-62273-585-3

Cover design by Vernon Press using elements by Chevanon / Freepik.

Product and company names mentioned in this work are the trademarks of their respective owners. While every care has been taken in preparing this work, neither the authors nor Vernon Art and Science Inc. may be held responsible for any loss or damage caused or alleged to be caused directly or indirectly by the information contained in it.

Every effort has been made to trace all copyright holders, but if any have been inadvertently overlooked the publisher will be pleased to include any necessary credits in any subsequent reprint or edition.

Table of Contents

- CHAPTER 1 – SENTENCES ... 6
- PARTS OF SPEECH ... 7
- VERBS – PRESENT SIMPLE ... 19
- VERBS – PAST SIMPLE ... 21
- ADJECTIVES ... 29
- ADVERBS ... 32
- CLAUSES AND SENTENCES ... 37
- SENTENCE STRUCTURE ... 37
- WORD ORDER ... 39
- SENTENCES AND FRAGMENTS ... 41
- SIMPLE, COMPOUND AND COMPLEX SENTENCES ... 44
- SUBJECT–VERB AGREEMENT ... 47
- CONDITIONALS ... 50
- CHAPTER 2 – PARAGRAPHS ... 53
- THE PARAGRAPH ... 54
- PARAGRAPH ELEMENTS – TOPIC SENTENCE AND SUPPORTING SENTENCES ... 59
- PARAGRAPH ELEMENTS – UNITY AND COHERENCE ... 65
- PARAGRAPH DEVELOPMENT – PARAPHRASING ... 78
- NARRATIVE PARAGRAPHS ... 84
- EXPLANATORY PARAGRAPHS ... 85
- COMPARISON PARAGRAPHS ... 89
- ARGUMENTATIVE PARAGRAPHS ... 91
- DESCRIBING VERSUS DISCUSSING ... 99
- WRITING ARGUMENTATIVE PARAPGRAPHS ... 113
- WRITING REFLECTIVE PARAGRAPHS ... 116
- CHAPTER 3 – ESSAYS ... 121
- THE ESSAY ... 122
- ESSAY DEVELOPMENT ... 127
- CITE EVIDENCE ... 139
- HOW TO READ A TASK ... 149
- PRACTICE WRITING ARGUMENTATIVE ESSAYS ... 161
- PRACTICE WRITING COMPARISON ESSAYS ... 179
- REFLECT. SHARE. WRITE. ... 187
- CHAPTER 1 REFERENCES ... 199
- CHAPTER 2 REFERENCES ... 200
- CHAPTER 3 REFERENCES ... 201

CHAPTER 1–SENTENCES

In this chapter, you will learn:

- ✓ *about parts of speech and word order in English sentences*
- ✓ *the difference between sentence and fragment*
- ✓ *the importance of subject-verb agreement*
- ✓ *different types of sentences*

PARTS OF SPEECH

There are four major parts of speech in English: **nouns**, **verbs**, **adjectives** and **adverbs**. Other parts of speech include *pronouns, prepositions, conjunctions, determiners,* and *interjections*.

- Nouns refer to persons, things, and animals.
- Verbs refer to actions, events, and states.
- Adjectives describe nouns, and adverbs describe verbs.

NOUNS

Nouns can be either **count** or **noncount**. Count nouns have both singular and plural forms (*book/books, teacher/teachers, task/tasks*). Irregular nouns change their forms in the plural (*woman/women, child/children, life/lives*). In their singular forms, nouns are used together with the indefinite article *a* or *an*. Noncount nouns do not have plural forms (*information, knowledge, news*).

In addition, nouns can be either **common** or **proper**. Common nouns refer to people or things in general (*phone, country, week*). Proper nouns are the names of persons, places or things (*Jane, Australia, Friday*). Proper nouns in English are written with capital letters.

Nouns can also be **concrete** or **abstract**. Concrete nouns refer to physical people or things (*computer, notebook, desk*). Abstract nouns refer to ideas, concepts, and conditions that cannot be touched or seen (*happiness, imagination, thought*).

Finally, nouns can be **collective**, referring to groups of people or things (*government, family, staff*). In American English, most collective nouns are singular, and thus have a singular verb. In British English, however, both singular and plural forms are used. Examples: *My family has a long history of depression. My family have a long history of depression.* (Both are correct.)

1. ACTIVITY—IDENTIFY SINGULAR AND PLURAL NOUNS

The sentences below are based on sentences from "Narrative of the Life of Frederick Douglass, an American Slave."

a. Find in the text the plural form of the nouns in the box. Compare with a classmate.

> trick, year, duty, soul

b. Find in the text the singular form of the nouns in the box. Compare with a classmate.

I lived in Master Hugh's family about seven years. During this time, I succeeded in learning to read and write. In doing this, I had to resort to various tricks. I had no regular teacher. My mistress kindly started to instruct me. But she stopped at the advice of her husband. My mistress was a kind and tender-hearted woman. She treated me as one human being should treat another. But she had to do the duties of a slaveholder too. Slavery proved as harmful to her as it did to me. When I went there, she was a kindhearted woman. There was no sorrow or suffering for which she had not a tear. She had bread for the hungry, clothes for the naked, and compassion for all souls that she met. But slavery changed her ability to act so generously. Under the influence of slavery, her tender heart became stone. Her warm temperament changed into a terrible brutality.

> families, times, teachers, mistresses, women, husbands, beings, slaveholders, sorrows, sufferings, tears, abilities, influences, hearts stones, temperaments brutalities

Answer

I lived in Master Hugh's **family** about seven **years**. During this **time**, I succeeded in learning to read and write. In doing this, I had to resort to various **tricks**. I had no regular **teacher**. My **mistress** kindly started to instruct me. But she stopped at the advice of her **husband**. My mistress was a kind and tender-hearted **woman**. She treated me as one human **being** should treat another. But she had to do the **duties** of a **slaveholder** too. Slavery proved as harmful to her as it did to me. When I went there, she was a kindhearted woman. There was no **sorrow** or **suffering** for which she had not a **tear**. She had bread for the hungry, clothes for the naked, and compassion for all **souls** that she met. But slavery changed her **ability** to act so generously. Under the **influence** of slavery, her tender **heart** became **stone**. Her warm **temperament** changed into a terrible **brutality**.

2. ACTIVITY–USE NOUNS TO COMPLETE SENTENCES

a. Complete the sentences below with the nouns in the box. Compare with a classmate.

> support, society, cities, progress, soldiers, events, country, rights, changes, radio, film, wages, alcohol, decade, war, laborers, chance, conditions, affairs, strikes

The 1920s in the United States are largely marked by two major (1) _____: the end of World War I and the Wall Street Crash, which sent the (2) _____ into the Great Depression (1929-1939). These two events speeded (3) _____ that were happening much earlier in the American (4) _____. The introduction of new mass communications, such as (5) _____ and (6) _____, together with female suffrage and the prohibition of (7) _____, made the (8) _____ different from others. However, there was a certain tension in the American society, which was known for celebrating both (9) _____ and tradition. After the (10) _____, the nation was spiritually tired, hoping for a (11) _____ to follow private projects and forget about public (12) _____. But postwar labor was experiencing a lack of (13) _____ from the government, which favored business interests over workers' (14) _____. This led to a long series of (15) _____ in which labor demanded higher (16) _____ and better working (17) _____. This caused an important population change – relocated farmers, returned (18) _____, and unskilled (19) _____ moved into (20) _____ that were becoming overcrowded.

Answer

The 1920s in the United States are largely marked by two major **events**: the end of World War I and the Wall Street Crash, which sent the **country** into the Great Depression (1929-1939). These two events speeded **changes** that were happening much earlier in the American **society**. The introduction of new mass communications, such as **radio** and **film**, together with female suffrage and the prohibition of **alcohol**, made the **decade** different from others. However, there was a certain tension in the American society, which was known for celebrating both **progress** and tradition. After the **war**, the nation was spiritually tired, hoping for a **chance** to follow private projects and forget about public **affairs**. But postwar labor was experiencing a lack of **support** from the government, which favored business interests over workers' **rights**. This led to a long series of **strikes** in which labor demanded higher **wages** and better working **conditions**. This caused an important population change – relocated farmers, returned **soldiers**, and unskilled **laborers** moved into **cities** that were becoming overcrowded.

9

b. Complete the sentences below with the nouns in the box. Compare with a classmate.

Nevertheless, for most Americans, the 1920s was a decade of (1) _____. They experienced a new (2) _____ of living, and new technological advances. The (3) _____ in individual income contributed to increased purchasing power for many Americans. American (4) _____ F. Scott Fitzgerald's (5) _____ "The Great Gatsby," reveals how Americans went on one of the largest splurges in (6) _____. The old American work (7) _____ changed from saving to buying as much as possible. There was a general (8) _____ among Americans that this prosperity would continue. This motivated both (9) _____ and (10) _____ to take financial risks. Americans could, for instance, buy (11) _____, television sets, (12) _____, or washing machines on (13) _____. This contrasted with the times before the 1920s, when Americans in general owned very few (14) _____, saved most of their (15) _____, which they spent only on essential (16) _____, such as (17) _____, basic clothing, and (18) _____. This (19) _____ marked the birth of a consumer (20) _____, in which the advertising (21) _____ was encouraging mass (22) _____ and mass consumption by telling the (23) _____ that they really needed all those goods. The advertising industry was telling Americans that they were offering them their (24) _____.

> faith, money, dreams, businesses, industry, writer, standard, individuals, pianos, ethic, rent, possessions, prosperity, public, production, boom, credit, history, novel, cars, period, things, food, nation

Answer

Nevertheless, for most Americans, the 1920s was a decade of **prosperity**. They experienced a new **standard** of living, and new technological advances. The **boom** in individual income contributed to increased purchasing power for many Americans. American **writer** F. Scott Fitzgerald's **novel** "The Great Gatsby," reveals how Americans went on one of the largest splurges in **history**. The old American work **ethic** changed from saving to buying as much as possible. There was a general **faith** among Americans that this prosperity will continue. This motivated both **individuals** and **businesses** to take financial risks. Americans could, for instance, buy **cars**, television sets, **pianos**, or washing machines on **credit**. This contrasted with the times before the 1920s, when Americans in general owned very few **possessions**, saved most of their **money**, which they spent only on essential **things**, such as **food**, basic clothing, and **rent**. This **period** marked the birth of a consumer **nation**, in which the advertising **industry** was encouraging mass **production** and mass consumption by telling the **public** that they really needed all those goods. The advertising industry was telling Americans that they were offering them their **dreams**.

3. ACTIVITY–IDENTIFY CONCRETE AND ABSTRACT NOUNS

a. Find nouns in the text below and sort them into concrete and abstract. Compare with a classmate.

Oscar Wilde (1854-1900) was a popular Irish writer, poet, and playwright. He was the son of a well-known surgeon in Dublin, and of a mother with literary ambitions. He studied at Trinity College, Dublin and then at Oxford. He was a brilliant student, and he spent eight years at universities, which made him into one of the most important intellectuals in history. Wilde identified himself with the aesthetic movement, a product of the eighteen-seventies in Britain. He used to wear glamorous costumes and search exquisite sensations. The aesthetic movement broke with the conservative Victorian traditions of excess and materialism. It praised the search for beauty and self-expression. It also emphasized quality in art over moral restrictions. Oscar Wilde believed that art should be pursued for its own sake and be part of daily life.

> **Answer**
> Concrete nouns: writer, poet, playwright, son, father, mother, college, student, years, universities, intellectuals, history, costumes; Abstract nouns: ambitions, movement, product, sensations, traditions, materialism, beauty, self-expression, quality, art, restrictions, life

b. Locate at least twenty nouns in the following passage from "The Picture of Dorian Gray" by Oscar Wilde. Sort them into concrete and abstract nouns. Compare with a classmate.

Upon my word, Basil, I didn't know you were so vain; and I really can't see any resemblance between you, with your rugged strong face and your coal-black hair, and this young Adonis, who looks as if he was made out of ivory and rose-leaves. Why, my dear Basil, he is a Narcissus, and you— well, of course you have an intellectual expression, and all that. But beauty, real beauty, ends where an intellectual expression begins. Intellect is in itself a mode of exaggeration, and destroys the harmony of any face. The moment one sits down to think, one becomes all nose, or all forehead, or something horrid. Look at the successful men in any of the learned professions. How perfectly hideous they are! Except, of course, in the Church. But then in the Church they don't think. A bishop keeps on saying at the age of eighty what he was told to say when he was a boy of eighteen, and as a natural consequence he always looks absolutely delightful. Your mysterious young friend, whose name you have never told me, but whose picture really fascinates me, never thinks. I feel quite sure of that. He is some brainless, beautiful creature, who should be always here in winter when we have no flowers to look at, and always here in summer when we want something to chill our intelligence. Don't flatter yourself, Basil: you are not in the least like him.

> **Answer**
> Concrete nouns: face, hair, ivory, rose-leaves, nose, forehead, men, church, bishop, boy, friend, picture, creature;
> Abstract nouns: beauty, intellect, exaggeration, harmony, moment, professions, age, consequence, name, intelligence

c. **Discuss in class.**

> ➢ Is "resemblance" a concrete or an abstract noun?

4. ACTIVITY–REFLECT

a. **Discuss in groups.**

1. Is *beauty* a concrete or an abstract noun?
2. Is *expression* in "an intellectual expression" a concrete or abstract noun?
3. Is *tradition* a concrete or an abstract noun?
4. Is *materialism* a concrete or an abstract noun?

b. **Write down your answers to the questions above.**

5. ACTIVITY–REFLECT

a. **Write two to three sentences in which you agree or disagree with the statement below.**

Beauty and intelligence are incompatible.

> incompatible
> mismatched
> conflicting
> contradictory

b. **Share your answers with the class.**

> **Suggested answer**
> People often perceive intellect and beauty as separate phenomena. When a person is beautiful, he or she receives a lot of attention and special treatment from other people. Beautiful people then learn that they do not need to work hard to get ahead.

6. ACTIVITY–COMPLETE SENTENCES WITH NOUNS

a. Complete the following sentences with the nouns in the box. Compare with a classmate.

> role, values, expectations, behavior, reasons, responsibility, emotion, shame, code, society, people, regret, standards

Guilt is a painful (1) _____. It is closely associated with (2) _____. Guilt is caused by the sense that you have done something wrong. It is based on the feeling of (3) _____ for something you should not have done. But even if guilt is a very painful emotion, it guides our moral (4) _____. In fact, guilt helps us develop a sense of right and wrong. Different (5) _____ feel guilty for different (6) _____ . This also means that people have different moral (7) _____ of what is right or wrong. Guilt is also connected to feelings of (8) _____ and sorrow, as well as humiliation. When we feel guilty, we have a sense that we failed to live up to the moral standards of the (9) _____. But our inner (10) _____ play a big (11) _____ as well. Guilt is also based on what we believe are other people's (12) _____ of us. Besides, it is also a means of telling us that we broke the (13) _____ of moral behavior.

Answer

Guilt is a painful **emotion**. It is closely associated with **shame**. Guilt is caused by the sense that you have done something wrong. It is based on the feeling of **responsibility** for something you should not have done. But even if guilt is a very painful emotion, it guides our moral **behavior**. In fact, guilt helps us develop a sense of right and wrong. Different **people** feel guilty for different **reasons**. This also means that people have different moral **values** of what is right or wrong. Guilt is also connected to feelings of **regret** and sorrow, as well as humiliation. When we feel guilty, we have a sense that we failed to live up to the moral standards of the **society**. But our inner **standards** play a big **role** as well. Guilt is also based on what we believe are other people's **expectations** of us. Besides, it is also a means of telling us that we broke the **code** of moral behavior.

b. Complete the sentences below with the nouns in the box. Compare with a classmate.

> hunger, feeling, childhood, result, train, survival, pain, emotion, knowledge, plane, decisions, fire, danger, people, risk, condition, actions, injury, fear, people

Fear is commonly defined as a (1) _____ of displeasure about the possibility of an unwanted event. Fear is considered by psychologists a primitive (2) _____, and along with anger, (3) _____ and (4) _____, is shared by both animals and

13

(5) _____. It is an emotion which influences a person's (6) _____ and behavior. Undeniably, fear is an important (7) _____ for survival. It represents the mind's reaction to an object or situation of pain or (8) _____. Fear relies on previous (9) _____ as basis to react to present experiences. Fear is learned in (10) _____, when one discovers the things that provoke pain, such as getting burned by the (11) _____ or getting injured from a fall. It is fear which makes us step back from the track of the (12) _____ or stay inside after reading about a storm coming. In fact, people who are easily frightened stand a better chance of (13) _____. In the evolution of the mind, (14) _____ became more and more accurate at assessing possible (15) _____, consequently making (16) _____ more rational. For example, travel poses always a (17) _____, be it by (18) _____ or (19) _____, but we cannot let fear prevent us from traveling. We cannot let it dictate our (20) _____.

Answer

Fear is commonly defined as a **feeling** of displeasure about the possibility of an unwanted event. Fear is considered by psychologists a primitive **emotion**, and along with anger, **pain** and **hunger**, is shared by both animals and **people**. It is an emotion which influences a person's **actions** and behavior. Undeniably, fear is an important **condition** for survival. It represents the mind's reaction to an object or situation of pain or **danger**. Fear relies on previous **knowledge** as basis to react to present experiences. Fear is learned in **childhood**, when one discovers the things that provoke pain, such as getting burned by the **fire** or getting injured from a fall. It is fear which makes us step back from the track of the **train** or stay inside after reading about a storm coming. In fact, people who are easily frightened stand a better chance of **survival**. In the evolution of the mind, **people** became more and more accurate at assessing possible **injury**, consequently making **fear** more rational. For example, travel poses always a **risk**, be it by **plane** or **train**, but we cannot let fear prevent us from traveling. We cannot let it dictate our **decisions**.

---

7. ACTIVITY–REFLECT

a. **Look up in the dictionary the words "overindulge" and "pamper". In groups, discuss the questions below.**

  1. What makes parents overindulge their children?
  2. Is a pampered child a pleasant child?
  3. Who models our personality?
  4. What is the best choice for parents: to control or to pamper their children?

b. **Choose two questions to answer in writing.**

Suggested answer

1. Parents love their children more than anything in the world. This makes them give in to their children's whims. We like to please the people we love. 2. A pampered child is never a pleasant child. A pampered child always expects his/her wishes to be met. Besides, pampered children think only about themselves and care very little about others, including their parents. 3. When we are babies, our parents have most influence on us. We talk and act by imitating them. When we start school, teachers and friends also shape our personality. 4. Ideally, parents should balance their behavior between controlling and pampering their children. Unfortunately, they either do the first or the second. Indeed, it is not easy to raise children, but if parents want their children to become responsible individuals, they need to teach them responsible behavior.

8. ACTIVITY–IDENTIFY SINGULAR AND PLURAL NOUNS

a. Find in the passage below the singular form of the nouns in the box. Compare with a classmate.

> writers, reformers, physicians, times, taboos, societies, teachers, behaviors, activities, expressions, fears, lives, responsibilities, freedoms, ways

b. Find in the passage below the plural form of each noun in the box. Compare with a classmate.

> norm, subject, school, year, attitude, person, youth, problem, age, child, parent, issue, interest

Havelock Ellis (1859-1939) was an English writer and social reformer. He was also a physician who studied human sexuality. Ellis challenged the norms of the time by discussing subjects considered taboo in Victorian society. He went to private schools in London, and worked as a teacher for four years in Australia. Havelock Ellis was interested in human sexual biology and behavior. He believed that sexual activity is a natural and healthy expression of love. Ellis thought it was important to change people's attitudes towards human sexuality. He tried to break up people's fear of talking about sex. Havelock Ellis also believed that youths should learn about mature life as early as possible. He thought it was important to think about adult problems at a young age. It is important that people have the courage to accept the facts of life in their youth, and it is the parents' responsibility to guide their children. Besides, parents should give their children the freedom to think for themselves about important issues. Unfortunately, fathers and mothers tend to be either too controlling or too unconcerned with their children. In the first case, they want to decide everything for their children. They want their offspring to be just like them, to think and act in the same way. Secondly, parents are concerned with pleasing their children. They live through their kids, and do not want to upset them. But instead of giving them freedom, they, in fact, encourage them to be stubborn and self-centered.

Answer

Havelock Ellis (1859-1939) was an English writer and social reformer. He was also a physician who studied human sexuality. Ellis challenged the norms of the time by discussing subjects considered taboo in the Victorian society. He went to private schools in London, and worked as a teacher for four years in Australia. Havelock Ellis was interested in human sexual biology and behavior. He believed that sexual activity is a natural and healthy expression of love. Ellis thought it was important to change people's attitudes towards human sexuality. He tried to break up people's fear to talk about sex. Havelock Ellis also believed that youths should learn about mature life as early as possible. He thought important to think about problems in young ages. Indeed, it is important that people have the courage and accept the facts of life in their youth. And it is the parents' responsibility to guide their children. Besides, parents should give their children the freedom to think for themselves about important issues. Unfortunately, parents tend to be either too controlling or too unconcerned. In the first case, parents want to decide everything about their children. They want their offspring to be just like them, to think and act in the same way. In the second, parents are concerned with pleasing their children. They live through their children, and do not want to upset them. But instead of giving them freedom, they in fact encourage them to be stubborn and self-centered.

---

c. **Find in the following passage from "Little Essays of Love and Virtue" by Havelock Ellis the singular form of each noun in the box. Underline them. Compare with a classmate.**

> centuries, copies, anxieties, freedoms, children, over-indulgences

d. **Find in the same passage the plural form of each noun in the box. Underline them. Compare with a classmate.**

> book, caprice, tyrant, tendency, effect, class, child, parent, result, ideal

The twentieth century, as we know, has frequently been called "the century of the child." When, however, we turn to the books of Ellen Key, who has most largely and sympathetically taken this point of view, one asks oneself whether, after all, the child's century has brought much to the child. Ellen Key points out, with truth, that, even in our century, parents may for the most part be divided into two classes: those who act as if their children existed only for their benefit, and those who act as if they existed only for their children's benefit, the results, she adds being alike deplorable. The first group of parents tyrannise over the child, seek to destroy its individuality, exercise an arbitrary discipline too spasmodic to have any of the good effects of discipline and would model him into a copy of themselves, though really, she adds, it ought to pain them very much to see themselves exactly copied. The second group of parents may wish to model their children not after themselves but after their ideals, yet they differ chiefly from the first class by their over-indulgence, by their anxiety to pamper the child by yielding to all his caprices, and artificially protecting him from the natural results of those caprices. So, instead of learning freedom, he has merely acquired self-will. These parents do not indeed tyrannise over their children but they do worse; they train their children to be tyrants. Against these two tendencies of our century Ellen Key declares her own Alpha and Omega of the art of

16

education. Try to leave the child in peace, live your own life beautifully, nobly, temperately, and in so living you will sufficiently teach your children to live.

Answer

The twentieth century, as we know, has frequently been called "the century of the child." When, however, we turn to the books of Ellen Key, who has most largely and sympathetically taken this point of view, one asks oneself whether, after all, the child's century has brought much to the child. Ellen Key points out, with truth, that, even in our century, parents may for the most part be divided into two classes: those who act as if their children existed only for their benefit, and those who act as if they existed only for their children's benefit; the results, she adds, being alike deplorable. The first group of parents tyrannise over the child, seek to destroy its individuality, exercise an arbitrary discipline too spasmodic to have any of the good effects of discipline and would model him into a copy of themselves, though really, she adds, it ought to pain them very much to see themselves exactly copied. The second group of parents may wish to model their children not after themselves but after their ideals, yet they differ chiefly from the first class by their over-indulgence, by their anxiety to pamper the child by yielding to all his caprices, and artificially protecting him from the natural results of those caprices. So, that instead of learning freedom, he has merely acquired self-will. These parents do not indeed tyrannise over their children but they do worse: they train their children to be tyrants. Against these two tendencies of our century Ellen Key declares her own Alpha and Omega of the art of education. Try to leave the child in peace, live your own life beautifully, nobly, temperately, and in so living you will sufficiently teach your children to live.

---

9. ACTIVITY–REFLECT

a. Discuss in groups.

> Describe parents who behave as if their children existed only for their own benefit.

b. Write a few sentences in which you describe such parents.

Suggested answer

Parents that behave as if their children exist for their own benefit are parents who try to live their failed dreams through their children. They want their children to achieve all the dreams they haven't managed to attain themselves. They encourage their children to follow ambitions they had themselves when they were young but failed to pursue.

---

c. Discuss in groups.

> Describe parents who behave as if they exist only for their children's benefit.

d. Write a few sentences in which you describe such parents.

Suggested answer

Parents who behave as if they exist only for their children's benefit are parents who find it hard to say no to their kids. They satisfy all their children's wishes at the expense of their own. Besides, parents who live for their children's benefit are bad at establishing rules and taking responsibility for their jobs as parents.

e. **Discuss in groups.**

   ➤ When do children become tyrants of their parents?

f. **Write a few sentences in which you discuss situations when children become tyrants of their parents.**

> **Suggested answer**
> Children are irrational creatures, who have not developed morally yet. They are not able to control their impulses. When parents give in to their children's impulsive behaviors, children detect weakness, and learn to use that in their favor. In this way, parents are at the mercy of their children.

VERBS—PRESENT SIMPLE

Verbs are words that describe what a person or thing *does* or *is*, or what *happens*. In English, verbs are largely divided into regular and irregular verbs. Regular verbs form different tenses based on established patterns. Irregular verbs do not follow the same rules.

In the **present simple** tense, the basic form of a regular verb only changes in the 3rd person singular. Most verbs have -s to their basic forms (e.g., *learn/learns, write/writes, travel/travels*). Verbs that end with a vowel that is not e, have *–es* at the end (e.g., *do/does, echo/echoes, go/goes*). Verbs that end with -s, -z, -ch, -sh, and -x add *–es* at the end (e.g., *miss/misses, frizz/frizzes, watch/watches, rush/rushes, fix/fixes*). If the verb ends in a consonant plus -y, it changes the y into an i before adding -es (e.g., *study/studies, modify/modifies*). But if the verb ends in a vowel plus -y, we just add -s (e.g., *stay/stays, delay/delays*).

We use present simple when we write and talk about actions or events that happen *regularly, always, sometimes, often, never, daily, monthly, weekly, yearly,* etc.

I, you, we, you, they learn	I, you, we, you, they go	I, you, we, you, they miss
She, he, it learns	She, he, it goes	She, he, it misses
I, you, we, you, they rush	I, you, we, you, they study	I, you, we, you, they stay
She, he, it rushes	She, he, it studies	She, he, it stays

Present participles end with *–ing*, and are used to form continuous tenses. They are used together with an auxiliary verb, except when they function as **verbal nouns**. Examples: *Thinking is not the same thing as doing. Practicing writing is the only way to get better at it.*

PRESENT CONTINUOUS	PAST CONTINUOUS	PRESENT PERFECT CONTINOUS
I am learning You, we, they are learning She, he, it is learning	I, she, he, it was learning You, we, they were learning	I, you, we, they have been learning She, he, it has been learning

10. ACTIVITY–IDENTIFY VERBS IN THE PRESENT TENSE

Examine the following excerpt from "The Picture of Dorian Gray" by Oscar Wilde. Identify verbs in the present tense and underline them. Compare with a classmate.

I never approve or disapprove of anything now. It is an absurd attitude to take towards life. We are not sent into the world to air our moral prejudices. I never take any notice of what common people say, and I never interfere with what charming people do. If a personality fascinates me, whatever mode of expression that personality selects is absolutely delightful to me. Dorian Gray falls in love with a beautiful girl who acts Juliet, and proposes to marry her. Why not? You know I am not a champion of marriage. The real drawback to marriage is that it makes one unselfish. And unselfish people are colourless. They lack individuality. Still, there are certain temperaments that marriage makes more complex. They retain their egotism, and add to it many other egos. They are forced to have more than one life. They become more highly organised, and to be highly organised is, I should fancy, the object of man's existence. Besides, every experience is of value, and, whatever one may say against marriage, it is certainly an experience. I hope that Dorian Gray will make this girl his wife, passionately adore her for six months, and then suddenly become fascinated by someone else. He would be a wonderful study.

Answer

I never <u>approve</u> or <u>disapprove</u> of anything now. It <u>is</u> an absurd attitude to take towards life. We <u>are not sent</u> into the world to air our moral prejudices. I never <u>take</u> any notice of what common people <u>say</u>, and I never <u>interfere</u> with what charming people <u>do</u>. If a personality <u>fascinates</u> me, whatever mode of expression that personality <u>selects</u> <u>is</u> absolutely delightful to me. Dorian Gray <u>falls</u> in love with a beautiful girl who <u>acts</u> Juliet, and <u>proposes</u> to marry her. Why not? You <u>know</u> I <u>am not</u> a champion of marriage. The real drawback to marriage <u>is</u> that it <u>makes</u> one unselfish. And unselfish people <u>are</u> colourless. They <u>lack</u> individuality. Still, there <u>are</u> certain temperaments that marriage <u>makes</u> more complex. They <u>retain</u> their egotism, and <u>add</u> to it many other egos. They <u>are</u> forced to have more than one life. They <u>become</u> more highly organised, and to be highly organised <u>is</u>, I should fancy, the object of man's existence. Besides, every experience <u>is</u> of value, and, whatever one <u>may say</u> against marriage, it <u>is</u> certainly an experience. I <u>hope</u> that Dorian Gray will make this girl his wife, passionately adore her for six months, and then suddenly become fascinated by someone else. He would be a wonderful study.

11. ACTIVITY–REFLECT

a. **Discuss in groups what makes a *selfish* person different from a *generous* one.**

b. **Write a few sentences in which you contrast a *selfish* person with a *generous* person. Use the linking words from the box.**

> unlike, while, whereas

> **Suggested answer**
> While a selfish person thinks about himself first, a generous person looks out for other people. A generous person likes to give, whereas a selfish person likes to receive. Whilst a generous person prefers to make others happy, a selfish person finds his own happiness most important.

c. Discuss in groups.

   ➢ What makes *charming* people different from *colorless* ones?

d. Write a few sentences in which you contrast *charming* people with *colorless* ones.

> **Suggested answer**
> Unlike colorless people, charming people are interesting to talk to. Whereas colorless people have nothing special about them, charming individuals are exciting in the way they talk and behave. While colorless people have no social skills or original ideas, charming people know exactly what to say and how to please others.

VERBS–PAST SIMPLE

In the **past simple** tense, regular verbs are used by adding –ed to their infinitives (e.g., *talked, needed, invented*). Irregular verbs change their forms in the past simple (e.g., *wrote, spoke, made*).

Both in the past simple tense and past participle, regular verbs end in –ed (e.g., *wanted, practiced, worked*). Irregular verbs have different forms for past simple and past participle (e.g., *ran-run; drew-drawn; spoke-spoken*).

We use past simple when we write and talk about actions done and finished in the past, which happened *yesterday, last week, last month, last year, in 2005,* etc.

I, you, she, he, it, we, you, they learned	I, you, she, he, it, we, you, they went	I, you, she, he, it, we, you, they missed
I, you, she, he, it, we, you, they rushed	I, you, she, he, it, we, you, they studied	I, you, she, he, it, we, you, they stayed

12. ACTIVITY–REWRITE FROM PAST TO PRESENT

Study the following text adapted from "A Dream of Wild Bees" by Olive Schreiner. Rewrite it by changing the verbs from past to present tense. Follow the example. Compare with a classmate.

A mother sat alone at an open window. Voices of children came through the window. The children played under the acacia-trees. In and out of the room the bees flew with their legs yellow with pollen. She sat on a low chair before the table. She took her work from the great basket that stood before her on the table. She watched the needle go in and out. The noise of the children's voices became a murmur in her ears. She worked slowly and more slowly. Then the bees flew closer and closer to her head. Then she grew more and more drowsy. She laid her hand, with the stocking over it, on the edge of the table. Then she leaned her head upon it. The voices of the children outside grew more and more dreamy. They came now far, now near. Then she did not hear them, but she felt under her heart where the ninth child lay. She was bent forward and was sleeping now. With the bees flying about her head, she had a strange brain-picture. She thought the bees extended themselves out and became human creatures, and moved around her. Then one came to her softly, saying, "Let me lay my hand upon the side where the child sleeps. If I touch him he shall be as I."

Example: *A mother sits alone at an open window.*

Answer

A mother **sits** alone at an open window. Voices of children **come** through the window. The children **play** under the acacia-trees. In and out of the room the bees **fly** with their legs yellow with pollen. She **sits** on a low chair before the table. She **takes** her work from the great basket that **stands** before her on the table. She **watches** the needle go in and out. The noise of the children's voices **becomes** a murmur in her ears. She **works** slowly and more slowly. Then the bees **fly** closer and closer to her head. Then she **grows** more and more drowsy. She **lays** her hand, with the stocking over it, on the edge of the table. Then she **leans** her head upon it. The voices of the children outside **grow** more and more dreamy. They **come** now far, now near. Then she **does not hear** them, but she **feels** under her heart where the ninth child **lies**. She **is** bent forward and **is sleeping** now. With the bees flying about her head, she **has** a strange brain-picture. She **thinks** the bees **extend** themselves out and **become** human creatures, and **move** around her. Then one comes to her softly, saying, "Let me lay my hand upon the side where the child sleeps. If I touch him he shall be as I."

---

13. ACTIVITY–REWRITE FROM PRESENT TO PAST

a. **Rewrite the text by changing all verbs from present to past tense. Compare with a classmate.**

In the 1700s, the United States is mainly a country of farmers. It imports most of its manufactured goods from Great Britain. Farm life, however, is exhausting. Even the simple things require a lot of time and effort to do. The whole family works twelve hours a day just to meet the basic needs. All family members work to get food, and they generally weave clothes. After its independence from Britain (July 4, 1776), Americans want their new country to industrialize as well. However, the country does not have a reliable transportation system. Many Americans find it more practical to have their own land than work ten-twelve hours in a factory for one dollar a week. Even voices like those of Thomas Jefferson and Benjamin Franklin declare that it is better for the country to stay a nation of farmers. They claim that life and work in the city is harmful.

> **Answer**
>
> In the 1700s, the United States **was** mainly a country of farmers. It **imported** most of its manufactured goods from Great Britain. Farm life, however, **was** exhausting. Even the simple things **required** a lot of time and effort to do. The whole family **worked** twelve hours a day just to meet the basic needs. All family members **worked** to get food, and they generally **wove** clothes. After its independence from Britain (July 4, 1776), Americans **wanted** their new country to industrialize as well. However, the country **did** not have a reliable transportation system. Besides, many Americans **found** it more practical to get their own land than work ten-twelve hours in a factory for one dollar a week. Even voices like those of Thomas Jefferson and Benjamin Franklin **declared** that it **was** better for the country to stay a nation of farmers. They **claimed** that life and work in the city **was** harmful.

b. **Rewrite the text by changing all verbs from present to past tense. Compare with a classmate.**

The United States industrializes rapidly during the 1800s, and ultimately exceeds Britain's dominance. By 1900, the United States becomes the world's leading industrial manufacturer. Americans initiate various amazing technological inventions, such as the steamboat, the sewing machine, the tractor, and the typewriter. But the most important invention of the time is the use of electricity, which can be used for the operation of many devices both at home and in factories. Electricity also proves to be essential for the spread of communication tools, such as the telephone and telegraph. Electricity is later used in machines such as the motion picture projector and the computer. Due to Henry Ford's affordable automobile, personal transportation becomes accessible to the public for the first time in America.

> **Answer**
>
> The United States **industrialized** speedily during the 1800s, and ultimately exceeded Britain's dominance. By 1900, the United States **became** the world's leading industrial manufacturer. Americans **initiated** various amazing technological inventions, such as the steamboat, the sewing machine, the tractor, and the typewriter. But the most important invention of the time **was** the use of electricity, which **could** be used for the operation of many devices both at home and in factories. Electricity also **proved** to be essential for the spread of communication tools, such as the telephone and telegraph. Besides, electricity **was** later used in machines such as the motion picture projector and the computer. Due to Henry Ford's affordable automobile, personal transportation **became** accessible to the public for the first time in America.

TO BE and TO HAVE

The most frequent verbs in English are *be* and *have*. They are used both as main verbs and as auxiliaries – helping verbs.

PRESENT SIMPLE	PAST SIMPLE	PRESENT PERFECT	PAST PERFECT
I am You, we, they are She, he, it is	I, she, he, it was You, we, they were	I, you, we, they have been She, he, it has been	I, you, she, he, it, we, they had been
You, we, they have She, he, it has	I, you, she, he, it, we, they had	I, you, we, they have had She, he, it has had	I, you, she, he, it, we, they had had

More examples: *We are students now. We were students last year too. We have been students, so we know how hard exams can be. We had been students for two years before we joined the book club.*

14. ACTIVITY–USE *TO BE* IN THE PRESENT

Use simple present of the verb *to be* to complete the following sentences from "The Man-Made World" by Charlotte Perkins Gilman. Compare with a classmate.

Humanity (1) _____ not a thing made at once and unchangeable, but a stage of development. Our humanness (2) _____ seen to lie not so much in what we (3) _____ individually, as in our relations to one another. Even that individuality (4) _____ but the result of our relations to one another. It (5) _____ in what we do and how we do it, rather than in what we (6) _____. Taken separately and physically, we (7) _____ animals, genus homo. Taken socially and psychically, we (8) ___, in varying degree, human. Our real history lies in the development of this humanness. Woman's natural work as a female (9) _____ that of the mother. Man's natural work as a male (10) _____ that of the father, but human work covers all our life outside of these specialties. Every handicraft, every profession, every science, every art, all normal amusements and recreations, all government, education, religion; the whole living world of human achievement: all this (11) _____ human.

Answer

Humanity **is** not a thing made at once and unchangeable, but a stage of development. Our humanness **is** seen to lie not so much in what we **are** individually, as in our relations to one another. Even that individuality **is** but the result of our relations to one another. It **is** in what we do and how we do it, rather than in what we **are**. Taken separately and physically, we **are** animals, genus homo. Taken socially and psychically, we are, in varying degree, human. Our real history lies in the development of this humanness. Woman's natural work as a female **is** that of the mother. Man's natural work as a male **is** that of the father, but human work covers all our life outside of these specialties. Every handicraft, every profession, every science, every art, all normal amusements and recreations, all government, education, religion; the whole living world of human achievement: all this **is** human.

15. ACTIVITY–REFLECT

a. **Discuss in groups.**

Charlotte Perkins Gilman believes that we are human beings first, and man or woman second. Our identity should not be linked to our gender, but to our actions. Our identity is based on our relations with other people. Do you share her view?

b. **Write three to four sentences in which you reflect on her view.**

Suggested answer

Women have historically struggled to prove that they are not intellectually inferior to men. A woman was identified first and foremost with the role of mother or housewife. But this is unfair and unjust. Women should be judged based on their actions. All individuals, regardless of their sex or social status, should be defined by their attitudes and behaviors. We are all equal members of the social and political life.

16. ACTIVITY–VOCABULARY PRACTICE

Match the words on the left with their equivalents on the right. Compare with a classmate.

1. Renowned   a. welfare
2. Growth   b. pleased
3. Oppressed   c. thrown into
4. Content   d. annoyed
5. Tossed into   e. famous
6. Outraged   f. ill-treated
7. Formed   g. flourishing
8. Point out   h. development
9. Wellbeing   i. shaped
10. Thriving   j. call attention to

1. Renowned – famous
2. Growth - development
3. Oppressed - ill-treated
4. Content - pleased
5. Tossed into - thrown into
6. Outraged - annoyed
7. Formed – shaped
8. Point out - call attention to
9. Wellbeing - welfare
10. Thriving - flourishing

17. ACTIVITY–REFLECT

a. Discuss in groups.

1. When do we become outraged?
2. What is important for our wellbeing?
3. What makes women thrive?
4. What makes men thrive?

b. Choose two questions to answer in writing.

> **Suggested answer**
> 1. We are outraged when we feel we are treated unfairly. Outrage is connected to anger, and it shows that we are deeply upset because something is wrong. 2. Our wellbeing depends on our satisfaction with our life. We increase our wellbeing by being active, and by making a difference in our own life and in the life of others. 3. Women thrive when they are appreciated for their efforts. They especially thrive when they use their abilities to improve their own lives and the lives of those around them. 4. Men thrive when they feel in control and exert their influence at home and at work. This is true because historically men were dominant in all spheres of life.

18. ACTIVITY–USE *TO BE* IN THE PAST

Use the past simple tense of the verb *to be* to complete the following sentences. Compare with a classmate.

Charlotte Perkins Gilman (1860-1935) (1) _____ a renowned American feminist and writer. She (2) _____ convinced that life (3) _____ growth, and that women (4) _____ not allowed to grow at the time she lived and wrote. They could not fully develop as long as they (5) _____ dependent on men economically. Women (6) _____ oppressed by men, and the world she lived in (7) _____ a world created by men for men. They (8) _____ content to have women at home, doing domestic work and being absent from the political life. But the world (9) _____ a shared place, she claimed, and it (10) _____ made for both men and women to participate in all spheres of life. She thought that the contrast between the natural ideals of young women and the sad realities they (11) _____ tossed into (12) _____ intolerable. Gilman (13) _____ outraged by the way women's souls (14) _____ formed by their lives in the kitchen. She pointed out how important women's independence and work (15) _____ for their wellbeing and thriving. Her written achievements (16) _____ extraordinary. She is best known for her short story "The Yellow Wallpaper," but she believed that her most important book (17) _____ "Human Work," which (18) _____ published in 1904.

Answer

Charlotte Perkins Gilman (1860-1935) **was** a renowned American feminist and writer. She **was** convinced that life **was** growth, and that women **were** not allowed to grow at the time she lived and wrote. They could not fully develop as long as they **were** dependent on men economically. Women **were** oppressed by men, and the world she lived in **was** a world created by men for men. They **were** content to have women at home, doing domestic work and being absent from the political life. But the world **was** a shared place, she claimed, and it **was** made for both men and women to participate in all spheres of life. She thought that the contrast between the natural ideals of young women and the sad realities they **were** tossed into **were** intolerable. Indeed, Gilman **was** outraged by the way women's souls **were** formed by their lives in the kitchen. She pointed out how important women's independence and work **were** for their wellbeing and thriving. Her written achievements **were** extraordinary. She is best known for her short story "The Yellow Wallpaper," but she believed that her most important book **was** "Human Work," which **was** published in 1904.

19. ACTIVITY–FIND SYNONYMS

Study the following excerpt from the short story "An Ideal Family" by Katherine Mansfield. Find in the text synonyms for the verbs in the box. Compare with a classmate.

> walked in, thought, had taken, hadn't returned, adored, pardoned, had occurred, indulged, arrived

It had been a day like other days at the office. Nothing special had happened. Harold hadn't come back from lunch until close on four. Where had he been? What had he been up to? He wasn't going to let his father know. Old Mr. Neave had happened to be in the vestibule, saying good-bye to a caller, when Harold sauntered in, perfectly turned out as usual, cool, suave, smiling that peculiar little half-smile that women found so fascinating. Ah, Harold was too handsome, too handsome by far; that had been the trouble all along. No man had a right to such eyes, such lashes and such lips; it was uncanny. As for his mother, his sisters, and the servants, it was not too much to say they made a young god of him. They worshipped Harold, they forgave him everything; and he had needed some forgiving ever since the time when he was thirteen and he had stolen his mother's purse, taken the money, and hidden the purse in the cook's bedroom. But it wasn't only his family who spoiled Harold, he reflected, it was everybody; he had only to look and to smile and down they went before him.

Vocabulary Bites

Be up to something – *do something secret or wrong*
Vestibule – *hall or lobby*
Caller – *a person who makes a call or pays a visit*
Saunter – *walk in a slow, relaxed manner*
Suave – *(especially of a man) charming and confident*
Peculiar – *strange in an unpleasant way*
Uncanny – *strange and mysterious*

Answer

walked in - *sauntered in*; thought - *reflected*; had taken - *had stolen*; hadn't returned - *hadn't come back*; adored - *worshipped*; pardoned - *forgave*; had occurred - *had happened*, indulged - *spoiled*, arrived - *turned out*

20. ACTIVITY–REFLECT

a. Discuss in groups.

1. When do we think that somebody is handsome?
2. Is being a handsome man different from being a beautiful woman?
3. Why do handsome people make us like and forgive them more?

b. Reflect on one of the questions in writing.

Suggested answer

1. We usually describe somebody as handsome when we refer to their physical appearance. A handsome person has attractive features, such as harmonious face, smooth skin, slender figure, and maybe elegant clothes and body movements.
2. We tend to believe that beauty belongs to women. This is because women have historically been appreciated for their looks rather than their intellect. Therefore, we are inclined to consider handsome men rather feminine. Generally, a handsome man has a proportionate face, that is a harmonious distance between the eyes, nose, and forehead. This makes the face attractive. However, when it comes to beauty and attractiveness, there is no distinction between men and women.
3. We tend to like and forgive beautiful people because we get charmed by their attractiveness. Sometimes, we are aware of it, but most of the time we are not. Human beings are attracted by traits which are pleasant to the eye, and appeal to their sensual pleasures. Even if beauty is not a choice (hence, unfair), it reveals the human attraction to aesthetics.

ADJECTIVES

Adjectives are words that give extra information about nouns. They can be used in two positions. Adjectives used before nouns are called attributive. Examples: *All he ever wanted was to get a valuable education. By the end of the course, students are expected to write well-formed argumentative essays. Daily meaningful conversations with their parents were part of their education. After reading a book, you could always see Anna in deep thoughts. We learned to argue well because we used to have an interesting debate in class every week.*

Adjectives used after verbs such as *be, seem, look, grow, become* are known as **predicative adjectives**. Examples: *She looks younger than she is. She seems pleased with this course. They are wonderful parents. She has become good at writing after practicing daily.*

Most adjectives are **gradable**, they show that something has different degrees. The meaning of gradable adjectives can be changed by placing one or more adverbs in front of them. Examples: *We have had an amazingly interesting experience in New Zealand. I hate to admit that it had been a fairly boring lecture. Climate change has brought about extremely hot weather. Even today, Charles Dickens is acclaimed as a remarkably talented writer. In their negotiations, they happened to meet unusually modest businessmen. In her previous job, the company was run by awfully arrogant managers.*

ADJECTIVE CLAUSES

Many sentences in English include **adjective clauses**. They have a subject and verb and begin with the relative pronouns *who, whom, whose, that,* or *which,* or the relative adverbs *when, where,* or *why*. They are sentence fragments, which do not express a complete thought. Thus, adjective clauses cannot act alone as a sentence. Example: *He was the melancholic type, with big sad eyes, in search of something meaningful to do.*

21. ACTIVITY–IDENTIFY ADJECTIVES

Find in the excerpt from the novel "Little Women" by Louisa May Alcott at least forty adjectives. Also, identify three adjective phrases. Underline them. Compare with a classmate.

Margaret, the eldest of the four, was sixteen, and very pretty, being plump and fair, with large eyes, plenty of soft brown hair, a sweet mouth, and white hands. Fifteen-year-old Jo was very tall, thin, and brown. She had a decided mouth, a comical nose, and sharp, gray eyes, which appeared to see everything, and were by turns fierce, funny, or thoughtful. Her long, thick hair was her one beauty, but it was usually bundled into a net, to be out of her way. Jo had round shoulders, big hands and feet, a flyaway look to her clothes, and the uncomfortable appearance of a girl who was rapidly shooting up into a woman and didn't like it. Elizabeth, or Beth, as everyone called her, was a rosy, smooth-haired, bright-eyed girl of thirteen, with a shy manner, a timid voice, and a peaceful expression which was seldom disturbed. Her father called her 'Little Miss Tranquility', and the name suited her excellently, for she seemed to live in a happy world of her own, only venturing out to meet the few whom she trusted and loved. Amy, though the youngest, was a most important person, in her own opinion at least. A regular snow maiden, with blue eyes, and yellow hair curling on her shoulders, pale and slender, and always carrying herself like a young lady mindful of her manners.

Answer

Margaret, the eldest of the four, was sixteen, and very **pretty**, being **plump** and **fair**, with **large** eyes, plenty of **soft brown** hair, a **sweet** mouth, and **white** hands. **Fifteen-year-old** Jo was very **tall**, **thin**, and **brown**. She had a **decided** mouth, a **comical** nose, and **sharp**, **gray** eyes, <u>which appeared to see everything</u>, and were by turns **fierce**, **funny**, or **thoughtful**. Her **long**, **thick** hair was her **one** beauty, but it was usually bundled into a net, to be out of her way. Jo had **round** shoulders, **big** hands and feet, a **flyaway** look to her clothes, and the **uncomfortable** appearance of a girl <u>who was rapidly shooting up into a woman</u> and didn't like it. Elizabeth, or Beth, as everyone called her, was a **rosy**, **smooth-haired**, **bright-eyed** girl of thirteen, with a **shy** manner, a **timid** voice, and a **peaceful** expression <u>which was seldom disturbed</u>. Her father called her 'Little Miss Tranquility', and the name suited her excellently, for she seemed to live in a **happy** world of her own, only venturing out to meet the few whom she trusted and loved. Amy, though the **youngest**, was a most **important** person, in her own opinion at least. A **regular** snow maiden, with **blue** eyes, and **yellow** hair curling on her shoulders, **pale** and **slender**, and always carrying herself like a **young** lady **mindful** of her manners.

---

22. ACTIVITY–WRITE ABOUT YOURSELF

Write at least eight sentences in which you use at least ten adjectives to describe yourself and your family. Share in small groups.

23. ACTIVITY–IDENTIFY ADJECTIVE CLAUSES

Read the following excerpt adapted from "The Story of My Life" by Helen Keller. Identify four adjective clauses. Underline them. Compare with a classmate.

At the beginning, I was only a little mass of possibilities. It was my teacher who unfolded and developed them. When she came, everything about me breathed of love and joy and was full of meaning. She has never since let pass an opportunity to point out the beauty that is in everything. She never stopped trying in thought and action and example to make my life sweet and useful. It was my teacher's sympathy which made my first years of education so beautiful. It was because she seized the right moment to impart knowledge that made it so pleasant and acceptable to me. She realized that a child's mind is like a shallow river which ripples and dances merrily over the stony course of its education and reflects here a flower, there a bush, over there a cloud. Any teacher can take a child to the classroom, but not every teacher can make him learn.

Answer
who unfolded and developed them; which made my first years of education so beautiful; that made it so pleasant and acceptable to me; which ripples and dances merrily

24. ACTIVITY–REFLECT

a. **Write a few sentences.**

   Describe a teacher that is/was important in your education. Use at least six adjectives and at least two adjective clauses in your sentences.

b. **Share in groups.**

Suggested answer
In 9th grade I realized for the first time that I was very **good** at languages. It happened because of my **English** teacher **who saw me and appreciated me**. She was observant, **kind**, and **compassionate**. On the days when I was **sad**, she would notice it and come to me after classes to ask what was troubling me. I remember to this day how **pleased** and **honored** I used to feel. She was one of those rare teachers who make a **lifelong** impression on their students. They are the mentors **who see you and make you believe in yourself**.

31

ADVERBS

Adverbs give information about a verb, an adjective, or another adverb. Adverbs may have various meanings and functions, and they indicate time, place, manner, degree, frequency, and purpose (e.g. *early, there, rather, sometimes, consequently*). Two or more words which function as an adverb are called adverbial phrases (e.g. *as soon as possible, in a bit, quite well, in the daylight*).

Formal English sentences also contain **prepositional phrases**, which consist of a preposition and an object. They may also have other words in them, such as adjectives or adverbs. They may be located anywhere in the sentence. When used in the beginning of the sentence, they are followed by a comma. Examples: *In other words, we should read Santayana because he offers a sensible idea of the world and people's given place in it. To the whole world, it seemed a horrible thing to say. To tell you the truth, I never believed I could finish my project in time.*

ADVERB CLAUSES

Adverb clauses are groups of words functioning as adverbs. They describe verbs, adverbs and adjectives and refer to the *when, how, how much, why* or *under what conditions*. They usually start with a subordinating conjunction, such as *although, as soon as, because, even if*, etc.

25. ACTIVITY–IDENTIFY AND SORT ADVERBS

a. Find at least eight adverbs in the following excerpt from the short story "The Kiss" by Kate Chopin. Compare with a classmate.

It was still quite light out of doors, but inside, the room was full of deep shadows. Brantain sat in one of these shadows. The obscurity gave him courage to keep his eyes fastened as ardently as he liked upon the girl who sat in the firelight. She was very handsome, with a certain fine, rich coloring that belongs to the healthy brune type. She was quite composed, as she idly stroked the satiny coat of the cat that lay curled in her lap, and she occasionally sent a slow glance into the shadow where her companion sat. They were talking low, of indifferent things which plainly were not the things that occupied their thoughts. She knew that he loved her, a frank fellow without guile enough to conceal his feelings, and no desire to do so.

For two weeks, he had sought her society eagerly and persistently. She was confidently waiting for him to declare himself and she meant to accept him. The rather insignificant and unattractive Brantain was enormously rich; and she liked and required the entourage which wealth could give her. During one of the pauses between their talk of the last tea and the next reception the door opened and a young man entered whom Brantain knew quite well. The girl turned her face toward him. A stride or two brought him to her side, and bending over her chair - before she could suspect his intention, for she did not realize that he had not seen her visitor - he pressed an ardent, lingering kiss upon her lips. Brantain slowly arose; so did the girl arise, but quickly, and the newcomer stood between them, a little amusement and some defiance struggling with the confusion in his face.

b. Find nine adverb phrases. Compare with a classmate.

Answer

It was still quite light out of doors, but inside, the room was full of deep shadows. Brantain sat **in one of these shadows**. The obscurity gave him courage to keep his eyes fastened **as ardently as he liked** upon the girl who sat **in the firelight**. She was very very handsome, with a certain fine, rich coloring that belongs to the healthy brune type. She was quite composed, as she idly stroked the satiny coat of the cat that lay curled in her lap, and she occasionally sent a slow glance **into the shadow where her companion sat**. They were talking low, of indifferent things which plainly were not the things that occupied their thoughts. She knew that he loved her, a frank fellow without guile enough to conceal his feelings, and no desire to do so.

For two weeks, he had sought her society eagerly and persistently. She was confidently waiting for him to declare himself and she meant to accept him. The rather insignificant and unattractive Brantain was enormously rich; and she liked and required the entourage which wealth could give her. **During one of the pauses between their talk of the last tea and the next reception** the door opened and a young man entered whom Brantain knew quite well. The girl turned her face toward him. A stride or two brought him to **her side**, and bending over her chair - **before she could suspect his intention**, for she did not realize that he had not seen her visitor - he pressed an ardent, lingering kiss upon her lips. Brantain slowly arose; so did the girl arise, but quickly, and the newcomer stood **between them**, a little amusement and some defiance struggling with the confusion in his face.

CAPITALIZATION

In English, we always use capital letters in the following situations:

When we use capital letters	Examples
At the beginning of a sentence	*Literature offers the ultimate time travel experience.*
Names of persons, countries, continents, etc.	Winston Churchill, the United States of America, South America
Names of regions, cities, oceans, geographical formations, streets, etc.	California, London, the Pacific, the Himalayas, Wall Street
Names of organizations, languages, nationalities, etc.	the United Nations, Norwegian, Italian
Titles of books, films, etc.	"Jane Eyre", "The Imitation Game"
Days of the week, months of the year, seasons, holidays	Monday, March, Spring, Easter

26. ACTIVITY–IDENTIFY CAPITALIZED WORDS

Underline all capitalized words in the sentences below. Compare with a classmate.

The Brontë sisters were born in Yorkshire, which is in the heart of England. In 1842, Charlotte and Emily went to Brussels. Their plan was to get familiar with French, and get some insight into other languages as well. In 1846, a volume of poems was published by Acton Bell, but they were not a success. These poems were republished after Charlotte Brontë achieved her first success, and people started to be curious about "Wuthering Heights." The history of "Jane Eyre," on the other hand, is that of a work which started a career, because it fell in the hands of the right man. The first story written by Charlotte Brontë, called "The Professor," had been rejected by many publishers. The novels of Emily and Anne Brontë were published soon after "Jane Eyre". They were issued in three volumes, "Wuthering Heights" occupying the first two.

27. ACTIVITY–IDENTIFY CAPITALIZATION MISTAKES

a. Find twenty-five capitalization mistakes in the following sentences taken from "Narrative of the Life of Frederick Douglass, an American Slave." Compare with a classmate.

i was born in tuckahoe, near hillsborough, and about twelve miles from easton, in talbot county, maryland. My mother was named harriet bailey. She was the daughter of isaac and betsey bailey, both colored, and quite dark. My mother was of a darker complexion than my grandmother or grandfather. She was hired by a Mr. stewart, who lived about twelve miles from my home. I have had two masters. My first master's name was anthony. I do not remember his first name. He was generally called captain anthony. He owned two or three farms, and about thirty slaves. His farms and slaves were under the care of an overseer. The overseer's name was plummer. mr. plummer was a miserable drunkard, and a savage monster. We sailed out of miles river for baltimore on a saturday morning. I remember only the day of the week. In the afternoon of that day, we reached annapolis, the capital of the State. It was the first large town that I had ever seen. It looked small compared with some new england factory villages. But I thought it a wonderful place for its size.

> **Answer**
> I was born in Tuckahoe, near Hillsborough, and about twelve miles from Easton, in Talbot county, Maryland. My mother was named Harriet Bailey. She was the daughter of Isaac and Betsey Bailey, both colored, and quite dark. My mother was of a darker complexion than my grandmother or grandfather. She was hired by a Mr. Stewart, who lived about twelve miles from my home. I have had two masters. My first master's name was Anthony. I do not remember his first name. He was generally called Captain Anthony. He owned two or three farms, and about thirty slaves. His farms and slaves were under the care of an overseer. The overseer's name was Plummer. Mr. Plummer was a miserable drunkard, and a savage monster. We sailed out of Miles River for Baltimore on a Saturday morning. I remember only the day of the week. In the afternoon of that day, we reached Annapolis, the capital of the State. It was the first large town that I had ever seen. It looked small compared with some New England factory villages. But I thought it a wonderful place for its size.

b. Find twenty-one capitalization mistakes in the following excerpt from "American Leaders and Heroes" by Wilbur F. Gordy. Compare with a classmate.

One of the most inspiring leaders who opposed slavery was abraham lincoln. He was born in kentucky, february 12, 1809. Little abe's only playmates were his sister sarah, two years older than himself, and his cousin, dennis hanks, who lived in the lincoln home. When abe was seven years old the family moved to indiana, and settled about fifteen miles north of the ohio river. Having arrived safely in november, all set vigorously to work to provide a shelter against the winter. Young abe was healthy, rugged, and active, and from early morning till late evening he worked with his father. He had but few books at his home, and found it impossible in that wild country to find many in any other homes. Among those which he read over and over again, while a boy, were "Æsop's Fables," "robinson crusoe," "pilgrim's progress." Just before he came of age his family, with all their possessions packed in a cart, moved again toward the west. For two weeks they travelled across the country into Illinois, and finally made a new home on the banks of the sangamon river, a stream flowing into the ohio. The tiresome journey was made in the month of march along muddy roads and over swollen streams, young lincoln driving the oxen.

Answer

One of the most inspiring leaders who opposed slavery was **A**braham Lincoln. He was born in **K**entucky, **F**ebruary 12, 1809. Little Abe's only playmates were his sister **S**arah, two years older than himself, and his cousin, **D**ennis **H**anks, who lived in the **L**incoln home. When Abe was seven years old the family moved to **I**ndiana, and settled about fifteen miles north of the **O**hio river. Having arrived safely in **N**ovember, all set vigorously to work to provide a shelter against the winter. Young Abe was healthy, rugged, and active, and from early morning till late evening he worked with his father. He had but few books at his home, and found it impossible in that wild country to find many in any other homes. Among those which he read over and over again, while a boy, were "**Æ**sop's Fables," "**R**obinson **C**rusoe," "**P**ilgrim's **P**rogress." Just before he came of age, his family, with all their possessions packed in a cart, moved again toward the **W**est. For two weeks they travelled across the country into Illinois, and finally made a new home on the banks of the **S**angamon river, a stream flowing into the **O**hio. The tiresome journey was made in the month of march along muddy roads and over swollen streams, young Lincoln driving the oxen.

28. ACTIVITY –WRITE ABOUT YOURSELF

a. Write at least ten sentences about yourself.

In your sentences, include details about:

- ✓ when and where you were born
- ✓ the names of your family members
- ✓ your nationality and native language
- ✓ your favorite book(s) and film(s)
- ✓ your favorite season(s)
- ✓ a country and city you want to visit

b. Share in groups.

CLAUSES AND SENTENCES

The basic unit of the English grammar is the **clause**, which consists of a subject and predicate. Examples: *while she was writing her assignment. But that was not his ultimate goal.* Clauses are made up of phrases, which are groups of words, but without a subject and verb. Examples: [while] [she] [was writing] [her assignment]. [But] [that] [was not] [his ultimate goal].

A complete sentence has a subject and predicate and expresses a complete thought or idea that makes sense. It often consists of more than one clause. It starts with a capital letter and ends with a period (declarative sentence), a question mark (interrogative sentence), or an exclamation mark (exclamatory sentence). Examples: *We are here to get an education. Why are you here? To get an education, of course!*

SENTENCE STRUCTURE

Simple sentences in English consist of a SUBJECT – someone or something that the sentence is about, a VERB – what the subject does or is, and an OBJECT – person or thing affected by the verb. Examples: *We need role models. English is a global language.* Subjects which consist of more than one noun are called compound subjects. Example: *The UK and the US are English-speaking countries.*

However, when sentences begin with *there is* or *there are*, the structure of the sentence is different. The subject is after the verb *is* or *are*. Examples: *There is a reason I am here.* The subject is *a reason*. *There are many reasons to be grateful.* The subject is *many reasons*.

29. ACTIVITY—IDENTITY SUBJECT AND VERB

Examine the following simple sentences. Identify the subject and the verb in each sentence. Compare with a classmate.

1. A good writer writes daily.
2. Barack Obama was the first black president.
3. Technological progress has changed how we work.
4. Most jobs require emotional skills.
5. More education offers better job opportunities.
6. Fame is no guarantee of happiness.
7. Reading stimulates imagination.
8. It is easy to blame others for our mistakes.
9. Nothing happens in a vacuum.
10. Learning is a lifelong affair.

Answer key (inverted on page):
1. **A good writer writes** daily.
2. **Barack Obama was** the first black president.
3. **Technological progress has changed** how we work.
4. **Most jobs** today **require** emotional skills.
5. **More education offers** better job opportunities.
6. **Fame is** no guarantee of happiness.
7. **Reading stimulates** imagination.
8. **It is** easy to blame others for our mistakes.
9. **Nothing happens** in a vacuum.
10. **Learning is** a lifelong affair.

30. ACTIVITY—FORM SENTENCES

Arrange the following words into complete sentences. Begin with the subject followed by the verb. Compare with a classmate.

1. advantages / many / to / language. / having / global / There / are / a
2. job / language / opportunities / A / global / offers / worldwide.
3. about / technology. / and / in / You / can / English / to / science / use / learn / discoveries
4. A / international / media. / access / language / gives / global / to
5. going / what / It / around / is / on / updates / world. / you / on / the
6. can / experiences / about / treatments. / use / Doctors / English / to / exchange
7. between / English / about / significant / countries. / issues / communication / simplifies
8. necessary / international / is / language / An / a / in / world / globalized

Answer key (inverted on page):
1. There are many advantages to having a global language.
2. A global language offers job opportunities worldwide.
3. You can use English to learn about discoveries in science and technology.
4. A global language gives access to international media.
5. It updates you on what is going on around the world.
6. Doctors can use English to exchange experiences about treatments.
7. English facilitates communication about significant issues between countries.
8. An international language is necessary in a globalized world.

WORD ORDER

To keep the **subject** and **object** apart in the sentence, we need to follow a certain word order. Most English sentences follow the following pattern:

SUBJECT	VERB	OBJECT
Children	like	bedtime stories.
Education	improves	the quality of life.

However, in sentences expressing somebody getting or being changed by something, we use indirect object + direct object:

SUBJECT	VERB	INDIRECT OBJECT	DIRECT OBJECT
A college degree	offers	young people	better jobs.
Dedicated teachers	motivate	students	to learn.
Good books	bring	me	great pleasure.

Numerous English sentences also contain **adverbials** found in various places in the sentence. Examples: *I always remind her of her duties, but she never listens. She rightly distinguishes between the philosopher and the poet. I purposefully left the first activity last.*

31. ACTIVITY–FORM SENTENCES WITH THE RIGHT WORD ORDER

a. Unscramble the following sentences by placing words in the right order. Compare with a classmate.

1. Franklin / in / is / Benjamin / a / figure / the / prominent / field / of / inventions.
2. prodigious / a / he / a / curious / mind. / with / was / inventor
3. list / Benjamin / long. / quite / of / is / Franklin's / The / inventions
4. the / He / stove, / is / of / inventor / fuel / improved / ventilations. / the Franklin / which / saved / and
5. He / the / of / founder / also / the / Philadelphia / is / Library.
6. In / the / post / of / the / addition, / Franklin / of / founder / system / is / office / America.
7. for / took / credit / But / his / he / inventions. / never
8. He / everybody / be / believed / should / charitable.

39

9. not / did / in / have / the / an / traditional / education / sense. / Franklin
10. intellectual / of / greatest / is / he / the / authorities / history. / one / But / in

Answer
1. Benjamin Franklin is a prominent figure in the field of inventions.
2. Indeed, he was a prodigious inventor with a curious mind.
3. The list of Benjamin Franklin's inventions is quite long.
4. He is the inventor of the Franklin stove, which saved fuel and improved ventilations.
5. He is also the founder of the Philadelphia Library.
6. In addition, Franklin is the founder of the post office system of America.
7. But he never took credit for his inventions.
8. He believed everybody should be charitable.
9. Franklin did not have an education in the traditional sense.
10. But he is one of the greatest intellectual authorities in history.

b. Unscramble the following sentences by placing words in the right order. Compare with a classmate.

1. heart / is. / the / where / Home / is
2. situations. / Fear / us / helps / avoid / dangerous
3. they / others / are / make / happy / when / happy. / People
4. to / world, / first. / change / you / want / change / the / If / yourself
5. You / are / for / every / you / choice / make. / responsible
6. world / Education / makes / the / peaceful. / more
7. To / understand / accept. / is / to
8. Some / never / people / change.
9. know / ourselves / We / others. / through
10. best / Books / friends. / our / are

Answer
1. Home is where the heart is.
2. Fear helps us avoid dangerous situations.
3. People are happy when they make others happy.
4. If you want to change the world, change yourself first.
5. You are responsible for every choice you make.
6. Education makes the world more peaceful.
7. To understand is to accept.
8. Some people never change.
9. We know ourselves through others.
10. Books are the best friends.

32. ACTIVITY–WRITE YOUR OWN SENTENCES

Write a few sentences.

Choose one of the sentences you have unscrambled in the previous activity that *you agree with*. Write at least five sentences in which you discuss your reasons.

SENTENCES AND FRAGMENTS

Sentences are groups of words that express **a complete thought**. When they fail to do so, they are fragments. Fragments do not make sense and are not grammatically correct. Examples: *He a strong passion for reading. (Fragment) He had a strong passion for reading. (Sentence) Even if worked hard, never managed to make his business successful. (Fragment) Even if he worked hard, he never managed to make his business successful. (Sentence)*

Present participle, or gerund, without a helping verb, does not function as a verb in the sentence. Examples: *An international language removing all communication barriers. (Fragment) An international language removes all communication barriers. (Sentence)*

A group of words that have a noun in place of a verb is a fragment, and not a sentence. Examples: *People could communication with each other and exchange their knowledge. (Fragment) People could communicate with each other and exchange their knowledge. (Sentence)*

33. ACTIVITY–CHANGE FRAGMENTS INTO SENTENCES

Read the following fragments adapted from "The Picture of Dorian Gray" by Oscar Wilde. Rewrite them into sentences using the words suggested in parentheses. Compare with a classmate.

1. There is no doubt that Genius longer than Beauty. (lasts)
2. That why we all to overeducate ourselves. (explains) (try)
3. In the wild struggle for existence, we something that endures. (want to have)
4. So, we our minds with rubbish and facts, in the silly hope of keeping our place. (fill)
5. The thoroughly well-informed man the modern ideal. (is)
6. And the mind of the thoroughly well-informed man a horrible thing. (is)
7. Like a shop with all kinds of monsters and dust. (It is)

Answer
There is no doubt that Genius lasts longer than Beauty. That explains why we all try to overeducate ourselves. In the wild struggle for existence, we want to have something that endures. So, we fill our minds with rubbish and facts, in the silly hope of keeping our place. The thoroughly well-informed man is the modern ideal. And the mind of the thoroughly well-informed man is a horrible thing. It is like a shop with all kinds of monsters and dust.

34. ACTIVITY–REWRITE FRAGMENTS INTO SENTENCES

Identify fragments among the sentences below. Change them into sentences by using the words in the box. Compare with a classmate.

> was / the man / born / he wanted / was / he / took / set up

1. American independence accomplished both by those fighting on and off the battlefield.
2. Who fought the struggle for independence with his influence was Benjamin Franklin.
3. Franklin born in Boston, the fifteenth child in a family of seventeen children.
4. His father was a candle-maker and soap-boiler, and Benjamin to become a clergyman.
5. Franklin's father sent the boy to school at the age of eight, but took him out again for lack of money.
6. At ten, he working in his father's shop, making candles, selling soap and acting as an errand boy.
7. He disliked his father's business, but was dutiful in doing everything his father asked him to do.
8. His diligence and passion for books and knowledge, compensated for his lack of schooling.
9. Spent most of his free time reading and saving money for a small library.
10. Benjamin was later sent to serve as an apprentice under his brother James at a printer in Boston.
11. In this way, Benjamin had access to more books and opportunities.
12. But the only time he could read was during the night.
13. At the age of seventeen, he a sailing boat to New York.
14. Having no friends and no money, he started looking for work in printing offices.

15. He later a printing business of his own, working from early morning till late at night to pay off the debt.

Answer
1. American independence **was** accomplished both by those fighting on and off the battle-field.
2. **The man** who fought the struggle for independence with his influence was Benjamin Franklin.
3. Franklin **was born** in Boston, the fifteenth child in a family of seventeen children.
4. His father was a candle-maker and soap-boiler, and **he wanted** Benjamin to become a clergyman.
5. Franklin's father sent the boy to school at the age of eight, but took him out again for lack of money.
6. At ten, he **was** working in his father's shop, making candles, selling soap and acting as an errand boy.
7. He disliked his father's business, but was dutiful in doing everything his father asked him to do.
8. His diligence and passion for books and knowledge compensated for his lack of schooling.
9. **He** spent most of his free time reading and saving money for a small library.
10. Benjamin was later sent to serve as an apprentice under his brother James at a printer in Boston.
11. In this way, Benjamin had access to more books and opportunities.
12. But the only time he could read was during the night.
13. At the age of seventeen, he **took** a sailing boat to New York.
14. Having no friends and no money, he started looking for work in printing offices.
15. He later **set up** a printing business of his own, working from early morning till late at night to pay off the debt.

SIMPLE, COMPOUND AND COMPLEX SENTENCES

A simple sentence in English is short and has a subject and a verb. It expresses a complete thought. Sometimes, a clause may act as a sentence, since a clause consists of a subject and a predicate. In this case, such a clause is considered independent, as it makes sense on its own. Examples: *I know. She speaks perfect English. She plays the piano at the weekend.*

However, in most cases, clauses cannot act on their own, which means they are subordinate. Therefore, they depend on other clauses to express a complete thought or idea. Examples: *but not Norwegian. but not during the week.* Most commonly, several clauses form compound or complex sentences. Examples: *She speaks perfect English, but not Norwegian. She plays the piano at the weekend, but not during the week.*

A compound sentence has more than one verb, and it consists of two or more independent sentences. They are connected with words such as *and*, *but,* and *so*. Sentences in a compound sentence stand independently from each other. Examples: *She speaks perfect English, but she does not speak Norwegian. She plays the piano at the weekend, but she does not play it during the week.*

A complex sentence consists of an independent sentence and one or more dependent sentences. They relate to words such as *while, when, even though, because, since*. They are called subordinating conjunctions. Examples: *Even though she speaks perfect English, she speaks no word of Norwegian. Because she works during the week, she plays the piano at the weekend.*

NB: Complex sentences indicate a richer and more varied writing than compound sentences.

35. ACTIVITY–IDENTIFY SIMPLE AND COMPOUND SENTENCES

a. **Examine the following sentences. Write S for simple sentences, and C for compound sentences. Follow the examples. Compare with a classmate.**

1. She loves literature but not physics. S
2. They had many friends, but nobody came when they needed help. C
3. When we help others, we also help ourselves.
4. Power attracts both men and women.
5. Everybody gets sad sometimes.
6. In a more globalized world, people become more open.
7. While studying, they also have part-time jobs.
8. He had no talent, so he worked harder than others.
9. Things are easy when you are a child.
10. Success is mainly based on perseverance.
11. They understand each other, but not always.
12. The Industrial Revolution started in Britain.
13. It completely changed the lives of the world population.
14. Most importantly, it transformed the nature of work.
15. The Industrial Revolution created a new relationship with time.
16. Many people moved to large cities, abandoning their farms.
17. Education is the best thing a person can get.

b. **Examine the following sentences. Write S for simple sentences, and C for compound sentences. Follow the examples. Compare with a classmate.**

1. When you focus too much on success, you forget to live. C
2. There are no beginnings or ends in history. S
3. Those who cannot enjoy leisure, cannot enjoy life.
4. Mental power, integrity and character are the results of school training.
5. Emotional intelligence is important both in school and in life.
6. If you use your will and act bravely, courage will replace your fear.
7. We learn habits in social environments, and they are like arts.
8. When we think too much about the past, we forget to live in the present.
9. Parental love is the most selfless feeling on earth.
10. For many, security is more important than freedom.
11. She had many dreams, so she worked hard to achieve them.
12. We are our genes, but also our environments.
13. They love the city, but chose the country because life is inexpensive there.
14. Both men and women find power appealing.
15. Women did not always have the educational rights they have today.
16. We like to think of the world today as a less unjust place.
17. Everybody should feel sad once in a while.

Answer a

1. She loves literature but not physics. S
2. They had many friends, but nobody came when they needed help. C
3. When we help others, we also help ourselves. C
4. Power attracts both men and women. S
5. Everybody gets sad sometimes. S
6. In a more globalized world, people become more open. S
7. While studying, they also have part-times jobs. S
8. He had no talent, so he worked harder than others. C
9. Things are easy when you are a child. C
10. Success is mainly based on perseverance. S
11. They understand each other, but not always. S
12. The Industrial Revolution started in Britain. S
13. It fully changed the lives of the world population. S
14. Most importantly, it changed completely the nature of work. S
15. The Industrial Revolution created a new relationship with time. S
16. Many people moved to large cities, abandoning their farms. S
17. Education is the best thing a person can get. S

Answer b

1. When you focus too much on success, you forget to live. C
2. There are no beginnings or ends in history. S
3. Those who cannot enjoy leisure, cannot enjoy life. C
4. Mental power, integrity and character are the results of school training. S
5. Emotional intelligence is important both in school and in life. S
6. If you use your will and act bravely, courage will replace your fear. C
7. We learn habits in social environments, and they are like arts. C
8. When we think too much about the past, we forget to live in the present. C
9. Parental love is the most selfless feeling on earth. S
10. For many, security is more important than freedom. S
11. She had many dreams, so she worked hard to achieve them. C
12. We are our genes, but also our environments. C
13. They love the city, but chose the country life because it is inexpensive there. C
14. Both men and women find power appealing. S
15. Women did not always have the educational rights they have today. S
16. We like to think of the world today as a less unjust place. S
17. Everybody should feel sad once in a while. S

SUBJECT–VERB AGREEMENT

One major rule of a sentence is that its subject should always agree with its verb. This means that a singular subject takes a singular verb and plural subjects are followed by plural verbs. Examples: *A school is a place of learning. Schools are places of learning.*

It is also important to remember that indefinite pronouns, such as *somebody, nobody, everybody, someone*, and *no one* take a singular verb. The same goes for verbal nouns, such as *saving, listening*, etc. Examples: *Everybody is present today. Nobody is immune to setbacks. Reflecting on one's own decisions is the quality of a responsible person.*

When a sentence includes a compound noun connected by *and*, the verb is plural. When a sentence includes a compound noun connected by *or*, the verb is singular. Example: *The teacher and the students are giving the same examples. His sister or his brother was a lawyer, I do not remember which.*

36. IDENTIFY SUBJECT-VERB AGREEMENT

Study the text below and underline subject and verb combinations. Follow the examples provided. Compare with a classmate.

<u>Interest is</u> the feeling and tendency to learn about <u>something or someone</u> that <u>excites</u> curiosity. When such a feeling is rewarded with a future pleasure, the interest continues. However, should there be disappointment, the interest declines. But what causes our interests? American psychologist and philosopher William James suggests that some things are *natively interesting* to us, they appeal to us on an instinctual level. According to James, the most natively interesting object to a person is their own personal self. Everything that has a direct connection to our own self becomes interesting. For example, you find a course in web design interesting because it will benefit you later in your further education or career. Similarly, a job seems exciting not because of its tasks, but because it offers you financial stability. In the same way, you find some of your friends interesting to talk to because of the feeling of camaraderie their friendships provide.

> **Answer**
> Interest is the feeling and tendency to learn about something or someone that excites curiosity. When such a feeling is rewarded with a future pleasure, the interest continues. However, should there be disappointment, the interest declines. But what causes our interests? American psychologist and philosopher William James suggests that some things are *natively interesting* to us, they appeal to us on an instinctual level. According to James, the most natively interesting object to a person is their own personal self. Everything that has a direct connection to our own self becomes interesting. For example, you find a course in web design interesting because it will benefit you later in your further education or career. A job seems exciting not because of its tasks, but because it offers you financial stability. In the same way, you find some of your friends interesting to talk to because of the feeling of camaraderie their friendships provide.

37. ACTIVITY—IDENTIFY SUBJECT-VERB AGREEMENT MISTAKES

Find subject-verb agreement mistakes in the paragraph below and correct them. Compare with a classmate.

John Lubbock tell us in his book "The Pleasures of Life" that ambition often takes the form of love of money. Few people try to make music, poetry or science, but most people does some kind of work to earn a living. Therefore, a bigger income are an enjoyable feeling of success. But there is always doubts about the benefits of wealth. Lubbock do not believe that people who is born rich are automatically happier. In fact, wealth need more work than poverty, and it certainly involve more anxiety. Of course, an income which grow with the years create a life of comfort. However, wealth have its problems, because money and the love of money often makes a pair. And as Ralph Waldo Emerson tell us in "The Conduct of Life", there is no use in being rich if one only hoards riches and constantly wish for more. Instead of being great proprietors, they become great beggars. And so, the more a man have, the more he want, so that the appetite for riches grow with wealth. In truth, it is often simpler to make money than to enjoy it.

> **Answer**
> John Lubbock **tells** us in his book "The Pleasures of Life" that ambition often takes the form of love of money. Indeed, few people try to make music, poetry or science, but most people **do** some kind of work to earn a living. Therefore, a bigger income **is** an enjoyable feeling of success. But there **are** always doubts about the benefits of wealth. Lubbock **does not believe** that people who **are** born rich are automatically happier. In fact, wealth **needs** more work than poverty, and it certainly **involves** more anxiety. Of course, an income which **grows** with the years **creates** a life of comfort. However, wealth **has** its problems, because money and the love of money often **make** a pair. And as Ralph Waldo Emerson **tells** us in "The Conduct of Life", there is no use in being rich if one only hoards riches and constantly **wishes** for more. Instead of being great proprietors, they become great beggars. And so, the more a man **has**, the more he **wants**, so that the appetite for riches **grows** with wealth. In truth, it is generally simpler to make money than to enjoy it.

38. ACTIVITY–IDENTIFY SUBJECT-VERB AGREEMENT

a. Study the text below taken from "What is Man?" by Mark Twain. Underline subject and verb combinations. Compare with a classmate.

From the cradle to the grave, during all his waking hours, the human being is under training. It is his human environment which influences his mind and his feelings, furnishes him his ideals, and sets him on his road and keeps him in it. If he leaves that road he will find himself shunned by the people whom he most loves and esteems, and whose approval he most values. He is a chameleon; by the law of his nature he takes the color of his place of resort. The influences about him create his preferences, his aversions, his politics, his tastes, his morals, his religion. He creates none of these things for himself. He thinks he does, but that is because he has not examined into the matter.

> **Answer**
> From the cradle to the grave, during all his waking hours, the human being is under training. It is his human environment which influences his mind and his feelings, furnishes him his ideals, and sets him on his road and keeps him in it. If he leaves that road he will find himself shunned by the people whom he most loves and esteems, and whose approval he most values. He is a chameleon; by the law of his nature he takes the color of his place of resort. The influences about him create his preferences, his aversions, his politics, his tastes, his morals, his religion. He creates none of these things for himself. He thinks he does, but that is because he has not examined into the matter.

b. Discuss in groups.

1. How do we know that we are created by our environment?
2. What are the consequences for being shunned by society?

39. ACTIVITY–USE THE RIGHT VERB FORMS

Complete the excerpt from "The Story of the Mind" by James Mark Baldwin with the right form of the verbs in parenthesis. Compare with a classmate.

We may say, then, that the man who (1) _____ (be) fit for social life must be born to learn. The need of learning is his essential need. It (2) _____ (come) upon him from his birth. Speech (3) _____ (be) the first great social function which he must learn, and with it all the varieties of verbal accomplishment: reading and writing. This (4) _____ (bring) to the front the great method of all his learning - imitation. All is learning; and learning not by himself and at random, but under the leading of the social conditions which (5) _____ (surround) him. Plasticity is his safety and the means of his progress. So he

(6) _____ (grow) into the social organization, (7) _____ (take) his place in the work of the world. These influences (8) _____ (differ) in different communities, as we so often remark. The Turk (9) _____ (learn) to live in a very different system of relations of "give and take" from ours, and ours differ as much from those of the Chinese. All that (10) _____ (be) characteristic of the race or tribe or group or family - all this (11) _____ (sink) into the child and youth by his simple presence in it, with the capacity to learn by imitation. The case (12) _____ (become) more interesting still when we (13) _____ (give) the matter another turn, and say that in this learning, all the members of society (14) _____ (agree); all must be born to learn the same things. They (15) _____ (enter) into the same social inheritance. This again (16) _____ (seem) like a very commonplace remark; but certain things (17) _____ (flow) from it. Each member of society (18) _____ (give) and gets the same set of social suggestions. The differences (19) _____ (be) the degree of progress each has made, and the degree of variation which each one (20) _____ (give) to what he has received.

Answer
1. the man who is 2. It comes 3. Speech is 4. This brings 5. the social conditions which surround him 6. he grows 7. he takes 8. These influences differ 9. The Turk learns 10. All that is 11. this sinks 12. The case becomes 13. we give 14. all the members of society agree 15. They enter 16. This again seems 17. things flow 18. Each member of society gives 19. The differences are 20. one gives

CONDITIONALS

We use conditional tenses when we speculate about how things *could be, could have been,* or we wish *would be.*

First conditional refers to present or future time and **real situations**. It indicates general truths. Examples: *If you practice regularly, you improve your writing skills. If you practice regularly, you will improve your writing skills.*

Second conditional is used in the past tense, but it refers to **present and unreal situations**. It indicates hypothetical conditions. Examples: *If I practiced regularly, I would improve my writing skills.*

Third conditional is used in the past perfect tense, and it refers to **unreal situations in the past.** It indicates past impossible conditions. Examples: *If I had practiced regularly, I would have improved my writing skills. If I hadn't practiced regularly, I wouldn't have improved my writing skills.*

40. ACTIVITY–IDENTIFY CONDITIONALS

Study the following excerpt from "The Story of an African Farm" by Olive Schreiner. Find conditionals and underline them. Compare with a classmate.

"But some women," said Waldo, "some women have power." She lifted her beautiful eyes to his face. "Power! Did you ever hear of men being asked whether other souls should have power or not? It is born in them. If Goethe had been a stolen away child, and reared in the depths of a German forest, do you think the world would have had "Faust"? But he would have been Goethe still— stronger, wiser than his fellows. At night, round their watch-fire, he would have chanted wild songs of rapine¹ and murder, till the dark faces about him were moved and trembled. His songs would have echoed on from father to son. Do you think if Napoleon had been born a woman that he would have been contented to give small tea-parties and talk small scandal? He would have risen, but the world would not have heard of him as it hears of him now— a man great and kingly with all his sins. He would have left one of those names that stain the leaf of every history— the names of women, who, having power, but being denied the right to exercise it openly, rule in the dark, covertly, through the men whose passions they feed on and by whom they climb.

> **Answer**
>
> "But some women," said Waldo, "some women have power." She lifted her beautiful eyes to his face. "Power! Did you ever hear of men being asked whether other souls should have power or not? It is born in them. <u>If Goethe had been a stolen away child, and reared in the depths of a German forest, do you think the world would have had "Faust"?</u> But he would have been Goethe still - stronger, wiser than his fellows. At night, round their watch-fire, he would have chanted wild songs of rapine¹ and murder, till the dark faces about him were moved and trembled. His songs would have echoed on from father to son. <u>Do you think if Napoleon had been born a woman that he would have been contented to give small tea-parties and talk small scandal?</u> He would have risen, but the world would not have heard of him as it hears of him now - a man great and kingly with all his sins. He would have left one of those names that stain the leaf of every history - the names of women, who, having power, but being denied the right to exercise it openly, rule in the dark, covertly, through the men whose passions they feed on and by whom they climb.

41. ACTIVITY–REFLECT

a. If you were given the choice of your sex, which would choose? Write at least four sentences in which you explain your choice. Use conditionals.

If I could decide my sex, I would choose to be…

b. Share in groups.

---

¹ rapine – robbing, looting, destruction

42. ACTIVITY–REFLECT

a. **Write four or five sentences in which you reflect on the following question:**

   ➢ If you could live anywhere in the world, where would you live?

b. **Share with the class.**

43. ACTIVITY–REFLECT

a. **Write four or five sentences in which you reflect on the following question:**

   ➢ If you were constantly watched, would you know who you really are (your actual thoughts and feelings)?

b. **Share with the class.**

44. ACTIVITY–REFLECT

a. **Write four or five sentences in which you reflect on the following question:**

   ➢ Would you know who you are if no other beings were around you?

b. **Share with the class.**

45. ACTIVITY–REFLECT

a. **Write four or five sentences in which you reflect on the following question:**

   ➢ If you had to choose between love or respect, which would you pick?

b. **Share with the class.**

CHAPTER 2–PARAGRAPHS

In this chapter, you will:

- *identify elements of a paragraph*
- *differentiate between different types of paragraphs*
- *practice writing paragraphs*

THE PARAGRAPH

A paragraph is a group of sentences expressing a single topic or idea. The topic or main idea – the topic sentence – is normally found in the first sentence of the paragraph, but not always. The rest of the sentences, called supporting sentences, are directly related to that idea. They develop, explain and offer examples which support the topic sentence. A paragraph cannot consist of only one or two sentences. Even though there is no fixed paragraph length, a paragraph should contain at least six sentences. Sometimes, paragraphs also have a concluding sentence.

PARAGRAPH EXAMPLE

Literature is the greatest medium to see the world through other people's eyes. It is certainly hard to know what it feels like to be a man, for example, when you are a woman, or how the life of a rich person is when you are poor. Of course, when we talk to other people we get glimpses into their views of the world. But people rarely share their most intimate thoughts and feelings in ordinary conversations. Literary characters, though, are more generous. They unreservedly impart their secrets, desires, doubts, and despairs with the reader. Indeed, the reader is the confidant who gains precious insights into their lives. In this way, readers transcend the limitations of their bodies and minds. They experience other lives which are distinctive (or maybe similar) to their own. Undoubtedly, witnessing life as others experience it must be the most precious quality of literature.

The topic of the paragraph is *Literature*. The main idea is: *Literature offers insights into how others experience the world.*

46. ACTIVITY–IDENTIFY MAIN IDEA

a. Study the following paragraph.

One of the first things we notice in all living beings is that "they are bundles of habits," declares American psychologist William James. Indeed, a large part of our lives is based on habits. They are as important as physiological functions such as breathing, digesting, seeing and walking. But while these functions are done instinctively, habits are learned and developed. According to John Dewey, we learn habits in social surroundings, and they are like arts. They need order, discipline and method. But no habit is independent of its environment. We develop our habits based on the social contexts of our lives. Dewey believes that habits are adjustments of our personal abilities to external factors. It follows that our habitual behavior is a combination of our individuality and external world. So, by changing our social and cultural environment, we also change our habits. However, we do not passively receive our habitual behaviors. We actively form them in a dynamic interaction with our environment and other people.

b. What is the main idea of the paragraph? Identify the topic sentence (hint: it is not the first) and underline it. Share with the class.

> Main idea: We form habits based on our abilities in combination with our environment.
> Topic sentence: But no habit is independent of its environment.

47. ACTIVITY–WRITE SENTENCES AND GROUP THEM

a. Answer the questions below by following the right sentence structure.

NB! In this task, you might want to use verbal nouns, e.g. <u>smoking</u> is a bad habit, <u>exercising</u> is a good habit.

1. When does something difficult become easy?
2. What makes a habit good or bad?
3. What are the habits of success at school?
4. What are the habits of success at work?
5. How can we make learning a habit?
6. How does a person become industrious?
7. How do we become very good at something?

b. Share your answers in groups.

c. **Group your sentences into a coherent paragraph that discusses habits. Begin the paragraph with the topic sentence suggested below. Use some of the linking words suggested.**

We are the sum of our habits, so we must be mindful of the habits that we make.

> To begin with, as a rule, for example, furthermore, besides, moreover, in fact, in truth, that is why

> **Suggested answer**
> We are the sum of our habits, and we must be mindful of the habits that we make. To begin with, when we talk about habits, we usually divide them into good and bad. As a rule, bad habits offer instant gratification, such as eating junk food or smoking. Good habits are generally those that offer future rewards, and which are harder to maintain, such as frequent exercising and eating healthily. For example, the good habits of a successful student are to attend classes, take notes, and study regularly. Being committed and engaged, working in teams and improving working routines are some of the habits of success at work. Furthermore, it is important to make learning a habit by challenging ourselves with new knowledge every day. We can do that by either talking to classmates or colleagues, or by participating in discussions in which people express different points of view from our own. Parents play a big role in teaching children hard work and discipline. Besides, being aware of our goals and dreams can motivate us to make efforts to achieve them. In truth, our wellbeing and success depend a lot on the types of habits we have. That is why it is so important to be watchful of the nature of our habits.

48. ACTIVITY–WRITE A PARAGRAPH

a. **Think about two or three habits that you have formed or changed when you changed your social environment. Think about *the reasons* why you have formed or changed these habits. Share your thoughts in groups.**

b. **Write a paragraph in which you discuss habits and change. Use the topic sentence provided to write a paragraph.**

We change our habits every time our life situation changes.

> **Suggested answer**
> We change our habits every time our life situation changes. Most habits are influenced by our parents, friends, classmates, teachers, colleagues, etc. It is therefore natural that we change habits whenever our life conditions change. When we are in school, we might be in the habit of studying for tests and exams on the weekend. When we have a job, we make sure we go to bed and get up early, with only weekends for relaxation. Besides, when we move from one place to a new one, our habits are the first to change. For example, we might walk to school or work instead of taking the bus, we might have an earlier lunch than we used to, we might do a different kind of sport because the weather is different. Thus, different circumstances require different habitual behaviors.

49. ACTIVITY–PLACE SENTENCES IN A PARAGRAPH

a. **Study the paragraph below.**

Change is easy when you change your habits. To begin with, people are no more and no less the sum of their habits as habits help us do things naturally. There are habits we can change with enough motivation and efforts, such as getting up early every morning to study or exercise. However, there are habits that are harder to eradicate, such as eating junk food or smoking. Indeed, some people are optimistic and others are pessimistic. Young people tend to be liberal while older people are more conservative. In the same way, educated people tend to be more open-minded than the less educated. In addition, effort, will power, and motivation are necessary elements of change. People form habits during a gradual process, and it takes time and patience to change them. But undeniably changing yourself starts with changing your habits.

b. **The sentences below are missing from the paragraph above. Identify their place in the paragraph. Compare with a classmate.**

1. But to change your habits, you must be aware of the habits that you have and wish to change them.
2. Besides, changing habits depends largely on people's mindset, educational background, and age.

Change is easy when you change your habits. **But to change your habits, you must be aware of the habits that you have and wish to change them.** There are habits we can change with enough motivation and efforts, such as getting up early every morning to study or exercise. However, there are habits that are harder to eradicate, such as eating junk food or smoking. **Besides, changing habits depends largely on people's mindset, educational background, and age.** Indeed, some people are optimistic and others are pessimistic. Young people tend to be liberal while older people are more conservative. In the same way, educated people tend to be more open-minded than the less educated. In addition, effort, will power, and motivation are necessary elements of change. People form habits during a gradual process, and it takes time and patience to change them. But undeniably changing yourself starts with changing your habits.

---

50. ACTIVITY–USE NOUNS TO COMPLETE PARAGRAPHS

a. **Complete the paragraph below with the appropriate nouns in the box.**

> everybody, poorhouses, building, worker, town, machines, children, factories, areas, workers, things, families

Even though child labor did not originate in the Industrial Revolution, it is in this time factories needed a great number of (1) _____ to perform simple tasks. This resulted in a huge number of children doing work in (2) _____ and mines. In early 19th-century Britain, (3) _____ as young as 10 years old entered factories, and in industrial (4) _____ children started work even earlier. An industrial British (5) _____ in the early nineteenth century would have a factory building near a river. Inside the factory, (6) _____ that make fabric are in endless motion. Each (7) _____ controls one or two of these machines. Young children race up and down the huge machines, fixing and changing (8) _____, like threads and bobbins. The factory owner goes around supervising, making sure (9) _____ does their part of the job. The children employed are from poor (10) _____, and the factory owner considers them lucky to work in his (11) _____. In this way, he protects them from the streets or the (12) _____.

b. **What is the main idea of the paragraph?**

c. **Share with the class.**

> 1. workers 2. factories 3. children 4. areas 5. town 6. machines 7. worker 8. things 9. everybody 10. families 11. building 12. poorhouses

51. ACTIVITY–VOCABULARY PRACTICE

Find synonyms for each word in the paragraph below. Compare with a classmate.

big, influence, completely, work, changes, changed, agrarian, automatic, caused, spread, upper-class, variety, consequences

The Industrial Revolution produced enormous social and economic transformations. It started in Great Britain in the late 1700s and took place during the 18th and 19th centuries. It refers to the changes from agricultural to mechanized societies, in which goods are manufactured in large numbers. Besides, it had a huge impact on the lives of the world population, as it radically changed the nature of work. It modified people's view of labor and created a new relationship with time. Besides, it gave the working class a voice through Trade Unions. Moreover, the Industrial Revolution changed the structure of social classes and the general standard of living. One major cause of the new way of life was the expansion of education in Britain. While the traditional school curriculum was designed for the aristocratic and middle-class elites, the new curriculum included a larger spectrum of social classes. Consequently, such transformations had large implications for the social and economic structures of the time.

(adjective) big – enormous, huge; (noun) influence – *impact*; (adverb) completely – *radically*; (noun) work – *labor*; (noun) changes – *transformations*; (verb) changed – *modified* ; (adjective) agrarian – *agricultural*; (adjective) automatic – *mechanized*; (verb) caused – produced, created; (noun) spread – *expansion*; (adjective) upper-class – *aristocratic*; (noun) variety – *spectrum*; (noun) consequences - *implications*

PARAGRAPH ELEMENTS – TOPIC SENTENCE AND SUPPORTING SENTENCES

The topic sentence is generally the first sentence in the paragraph. Occasionally, writers can position the topic sentence in the middle or even at the end of the paragraph. Paragraphs that tell a story or describe somebody or something do not always have a topic sentence, but they still have one main idea, and all sentences are centered around that idea. A topic sentence is never too general nor too specific, and it expresses an idea which can be discussed and not a fact.

Supporting sentences are related to the topic sentence or main idea of the paragraph. They include details, such as definitions, descriptions, explanations, facts and examples which clarify the main idea.

52. ACTIVITY–IDENTIFY GOOD TOPIC SENTENCES

a. Read the following sentences. Classify them into suitable and unsuitable topic sentences for *opinion paragraphs*.

1. Every year, one of every five deaths in the United States is caused by smoking.
2. Smokers should not have their cancer treatments covered by public money.
3. Talent is not something you are born with, it is something you develop.
4. R.K. Narayan is one of the most widely read Indian novelists who wrote in English.
5. The United Kingdom consists of England, Scotland, Wales and Northern Ireland.
6. Barack Obama was the first black president of the United States.
7. Oslo is the capital of Norway.
8. Many people did not have their expectations met during Barack Obama's presidency.
9. There is a mountain in Australia called Mountain Disappointment.
10. One million seconds is approximately eleven days.

b. Share with the class.

Good topic sentences
1. Smokers should not have their cancer treatments covered by public money.
2. Barack Obama was the first black president of the United States.
3. Many people did not have their expectations met during Barack Obama's presidency.

53. ACTIVITY–IDENTIFY THE TOPIC SENTENCE

a. **Study the following paragraph.**

When we read "Oliver Twist" by Charles Dickens, for example, we are transported to the Victorian era, and learn about the Victorian workhouses and London streets. When reading "A Cup of Tea" by Katherine Mansfield, we can witness how different the lives of the rich were from those of the poor. In the same way, when we read Sherwood Anderson's "The Egg," we observe another side of the 1920s in the US, in which the American dream is out of reach for many. In addition, literature helps us compare social issues in the past with those in the present. For example, Toni Morrison and Kate Chopin show us in their stories the terrible consequences of racial prejudice in the past and present America. Indeed, we would not be able to learn so many intimate details about the past had it not been for literature. Ultimately, literature teaches us that no matter the historical time, we all deal with what it means to be human.

b. **Choose the best suited topic sentence for the paragraph. Compare with a classmate.**

1. Reading Charles Dickens helps us understand Victorian society better.
2. Literature is the best time travel machine we have.
3. Toni Morrison's novels make us grasp the awfulness of racial prejudice.

Literature is the best time travel machine we have.

54. ACTIVITY–IDENTIFY TOPIC SENTENCE

a. **Study the following paragraph.**

Thus, it is important to develop the right habits for a good life. Aristotle suggests that well trained habits lead to happiness. Happiness, according to him, is to follow the principles of justice. This is easy to achieve once habits are formed, because good behaviors will need no energy or effort to perform. They become part of who we are. Therefore, happiness becomes a habitual exercise of virtuous behaviors, and we develop such behaviors by doing them often. We inevitably learn how to make things by making them. We also become just by doing just actions. We cannot become brave unless we engage in brave actions. According to the American philosopher and psychologist John Dewey, habits are our learned tendencies to react in different situations of life. Dewey claims that a habit is essentially will. For example, we do not become brave by avoiding dangerous situations. We become brave by exposing ourselves to risky situations and develop character by the way we react to danger.

   b. Choose a suitable topic sentence for the paragraph. Compare with a classmate.

   1. It is generally accepted that we become what we repeatedly do.
   2. We become brave by engaging in brave actions.
   3. We are happy when we are just.

> It is generally accepted that we become what we repeatedly do.

55. ACTIVITY–IDENTIFY THE RIGHT TOPIC SENTENCE

   a. Study the two paragraphs below.

1. _____

Of Scotch-Irish descent, Sherwood Anderson was born in 1876 in Camden, Ohio. His father used to be a harness-maker fond of horses. After losing his business, he started to drink heavily, which forced the three children and their mother to support the family. At different times, Anderson worked as a farmhand, as a grocery delivery boy, and as a newsboy, among many other odd jobs. He was in fact nicknamed by those who knew him 'Jobby', because of his willingness to do all kinds of jobs. However, despite his drinking, Anderson's father had a cheerful temperament and taught his children the love of music, theatre, and literature. This is why his father's character is present in many of Anderson's stories. The author's life ended in 1941 when he got sick with peritonitis on a ship to South America, where he was headed in order to escape the tensions of World War II.

2. _____

In fact, his narrative art was an early influence on Ernest Hemingway and William Faulkner. Sherwood Anderson's characters are individuals who are struggling to find purpose in a difficult world. Anderson was a serious thinker, largely concerned with the reality of the unconscious mind. He believed that the unconscious was a storage of the individual's secrets and his past experiences. His stories portray characters whose lives are full of sorrow, misunderstanding, and confusion. We can feel the author's genuine compassion for their suffering when we read his stories. He was also saddened by the plight of women in parts of the United States, which reminded him of his hardworking mother. Besides, Anderson was interested in the way the machine age and industrialism hurt people's spirit by depriving them of a sense of pride and achievement.

b. The two sentences below are the topic sentences of the paragraphs above. Match them with the right paragraph.

A. Sherwood Anderson, a largely self-educated writer, was a significant figure in the development of the American short story during the 1920s-1930s.
B. Sherwood Anderson was an American novelist and short story writer who used his childhood hardships in his writing.

1.B 2.A

56. ACTIVITY–STUDY A PARAGRAPH

a. Study the following paragraph.

A person who chooses the career of a nurse should possess some essential qualities. First of all, a good nurse should be compassionate, as empathy and patience are crucial to do and enjoy the work of a nurse. For example, when a patient gets angry, aggressive, or depressed, a nurse should be able to keep a balanced emotional state of mind. Next, a nurse should be a good communicator. To work well in teams, a nurse needs to communicate well, be flexible to change, as well as be open to learn from others. For instance, when you do not know how to deal with a task, you should be able to ask for help. Besides, whenever you have the chance to help a colleague in need, you should be willing to do so. Finally, a nurse is naturally helpful, as helping others is the most important part of the job. The nurse is the first person patients interact with when they need medical help. That is why it is essential that a nurse enjoys aiding those in need.

b. Discuss in groups.

1. What is the topic sentence of this paragraph?
2. How many qualities are mentioned in this paragraph? Circle them.
3. What are the details/examples used to explain those qualities? Underline them.

> a. A person who chooses the career of a nurse should possess some essential qualities.
>
> b. A person who chooses the career of a nurse should possess some essential qualities. First of all, a good nurse should be **compassionate**, as empathy and patience are crucial to do and enjoy the work of a nurse. For example, when a patient gets angry, aggressive, or depressed, a nurse should be able to keep a balanced emotional state of mind. Next, a nurse should be **a good communicator**. To work well in teams, a nurse needs to communicate well, be flexible to change, as well as be open to learn from others. For instance, when you do not know how to deal with a task, you should be able to ask for help. Besides, whenever you have the chance to help a colleague in need, you should be willing to do so. Finally, a nurse is naturally **helpful**, as helping others is the most important part of the job. The nurse is the first person patients interact with when they need medical help. That is why it is essential that a nurse enjoys aiding those in need.
>
> c. Compassionate, a good communicator, helpful.

57. ACTIVITY–WRITE A PARAGRAPH

a. **Discuss in groups.**

➢ What are the three most important qualities of a leader?

b. **Write a paragraph like the one in the previous activity.**

Discuss *the qualities of a leader* by following the same structure. Include three qualities a good leader should possess and give details and examples.

> **Suggested answer**
>
> A person who chooses to be a leader should possess some essential qualities. First of all, a good leader should be respectful. He or she should treat everybody in a polite manner, regardless of their culture, religion, etc. For example, a leader should be considerate of an employee who needs a day off, or show consideration for linguistic misunderstandings. Besides, a leader should be humble and concerned with the wellbeing of his/her employees. Next, a leader should be professional. A professional leader is aware of her/his position and she/he does not abuse it. Besides, a leader should have positive attitudes and should be reliable. For example, when employees need help, they should be able to get a fair and confidential treatment from their leader. Finally, a leader must be flexible, as she/he needs to adapt to different people and situations. A flexible leader is also creative and able to solve problems at short notice. In conclusion, the job of a leader is quite demanding and it is not the right job for everyone.

58. ACTIVITY–IDENTIFY SENTENCE ELEMENTS

a. **Study the following paragraph.**

Good writing is an important skill not only in school but in various fields of life. To begin with, writing helps structure your thoughts and make sense of daily impressions. Sometimes, when you jot down what you think or feel helps you understand your thoughts or feelings better. In addition, good writing skills are fundamental both when you look for a job and when you perform your job. For example, a well-written cover letter is the first impression your potential employer makes of you. Besides, writing e-mails, messages and reports is part of a working day for most employees today. Finally, writing helps you become a great communicator and enriches your vocabulary. For example, when you write, you feel the need to vary your language. You want to express yourself in a more nuanced and complex manner. There is no doubt that writing offers you a more organized and nuanced experience of the world.

b. Discuss in groups.

1. What is the topic sentence of the paragraph?
2. What are the three aspects of life in which writing is essential?

> 1. Good writing is an important skill not only in school but in various fields of life. 2. Writing helps understanding your thoughts. Writing is important when looking for and doing a job. Writing boosts communication skills.

59. ACTIVITY–REFLECT

a. In groups, make a list of the ways people can improve their writing skills.

b. Write a paragraph which starts with the following topic sentence:

We can learn to write well in various ways.

> **Suggested answer**
> We can learn to write well in various ways. To begin with, reading a lot is the first step towards good writing. When we read, we learn the structure of sentences and we improve our vocabulary. Also, by reading different kinds of texts, we learn how language is used in different contexts and for different purposes. Furthermore, writing is a matter of practice, one gets better at writing by doing it often. Therefore, it is important to make writing a habit. Asking for advice and guidance is also a great way to improve writing skills. Finally, writing, just like other skills, needs the right amount of determination and motivation. It is challenging at first, but it becomes easier when done frequently.

PARAGRAPH ELEMENTS–UNITY AND COHERENCE

The unity of a paragraph refers to all its sentences being related to one main idea. A paragraph has only one focus, thus one single thought. Every sentence in the paragraph should be connected to its central idea. Random sentences only confuse the reader and make a paragraph look chaotic and illogical. Also, a paragraph ends with the same central point that it started with.

The coherence of a paragraph refers to the details that help readers see how and why sentences are interconnected. In a coherent paragraph sentences are arranged in a logical order carrying the main idea throughout the paragraph. Coherence can be achieved in various ways, one of which is by using linking words.

Linking words indicate how everything makes sense, and how the main idea is transported smoothly from one sentence to the next. Besides, periodical use of synonyms is an efficient way to create coherence.

60. ACTIVITY–STUDY PARAGRAPH UNITY AND COHERENCE

a. **Study the following paragraph.**

How we make sense of our social world depends on contextual, cultural and motivational factors. Contextual considerations make us mindful of relevant information for specific situations. For example, when I attend a social science class, I am likely to pay attention to other students taking the same course. Also, if I am an introverted person, I might want to find someone who likes one-on-one conversations rather than large groups. Furthermore, we interpret our social world through culturally-tinted glasses. To illustrate, if I believe in gender equality, the gender of a leader, scientist or politician will not impact how I evaluate her competence. The same goes for the motivational factors, as my motivations will affect my behavior. For instance, if I am driven by the need for achievement, I will always see the world in terms of goals and tasks I can accomplish. This will influence how I interpret and respond in my interactions with other people.

b. **Does this paragraph have coherence and unity? Discuss in groups.**

c. **Can you give more examples of contextual, cultural and motivational factors?**

61. ACTIVITY–STUDY PARAGRAPH UNITY AND COHERENCE

a. **Study the following paragraph.**

Prejudice represents a negative attitude and a feeling of dislike about a group of people. Such an attitude is based on the beliefs that members of a group are ignorant or dangerous. But prejudice is much more complex than that. It can also include a condescending regard which keeps the victim underprivileged. The study of prejudice started with the study of racism in the 1920s. Yet, we know today that prejudice can be applied to different groups. For example, overweight people meet prejudiced attitudes whenever they look for a partner or a job, as they are considered less attractive and intelligent than other groups. Prejudice is often associated with discrimination, but the two should be distinguished. Prejudice is a hostile attitude, while discrimination is hostile behavior.

b. **Does this paragraph have coherence and unity? Discuss in groups.**

> The paragraph in activity 59 is coherent and has unity. It has a topic sentence and all supporting sentences are related to that sentence. The paragraph in activity 60 is partly coherent.

62. ACTIVITY–WRITE A TOPIC SENTENCE

a. **Examine the following paragraph.**

Love can be a burden and a curse, and instead of elevating the spirit, it can diminish it. One illustrative example is Somerset Maugham's novel "Of Human Bondage". In the novel, we read the story of Philip Carey, who struggles to find meaning in an indifferent world. He is pained at being unable to find someone to love and be loved in return. His love is not what he dreamt of, and it is a major source of misery and self-doubt. He falls in love with Mildred, a woman who contradicts everything he has ever imagined love is. She is shameless, vulgar and intellectually inferior to him in every respect. Philip's longing for a connection with Mildred becomes a painful obsession which impoverishes him, making him isolated and unhappy. He finds himself begging for love where no love could be found. The reader, just like Philip, feels indignation at this irrational and humiliating feeling. In fact,

Philip often laughs at himself when thinking about the days he longed to experience the power of love. All he ever wants now is to never have loved at all.

   b. **What is the main idea of the paragraph? Write a suitable topic sentence.**

   c. **Share in groups.**

> Main idea: Love is not always the best thing that can happen to us.
> Topic sentence: Love is not always virtuous and it is not always better to have loved than not.

63. ACTIVITY–IDENTIFY IRRELEVANT SENTENCE

Study the following paragraph and identify one sentence which breaks its unity. Compare with a classmate.

In the 1700s, the United States was mainly a country of farmers, importing most of its manufactured goods from Great Britain. Farm life, however, was exhausting, and even the simplest of objects required a lot of time and effort to do. Weaving clothes and getting food, for instance, required that the whole family worked twelve hours a day just to meet the basic needs. In Britain, people made great efforts to escape the harsh conditions of farming life. After its independence from Britain (July 4, 1776), Americans wanted their new country to industrialize as well. However, the country did not have a reliable transportation system, and for many Americans it seemed more practical to get some land of their own than work ten-twelve hours in a factory for one dollar a week. Even voices like those of Thomas Jefferson and Benjamin Franklin claimed that it was better for the country to stay a nation of farmers, and that life and work in the city was harmful.

> In Britain, people made great efforts to escape the harsh conditions of farming life.

64. ACTIVITY–EXAMINE PARAGRAPH UNITY

   a. **Study the following paragraph.**

The Gilded Age, which is the period following the American Civil War, was both a time of great prosperity and enormous poverty. The last three decades of the nineteenth century were the years in which American economy offered unparalleled opportunities to make great fortunes. Industrial magnates like Andrew Carnegie and John D. Rockefeller opened the way for corporate economy. Huge moguls had monopoly over the economy, and this resulted in the ruin of the small farmers who were unable to compete with the giant industrialists. This also meant that industrial workers and farmers had less economic and social security and were harshly exploited. Mark Twain, who coined the term in 1890, was a prominent figure who satirized the American society of the time. The term "gilded" indicated a society disguised in gold but with crudity and misery underneath the surface.

b. One of the sentences below belongs in the paragraph. Identify it and its place in the paragraph.

1. Mark Twain mocked the Gilded Age in his novel "The Gilded Age: A Tale of Today."
2. But this also set the scene for corruption and the ruin of a free-market economy.
3. Not everybody shared the new prosperity of the time.

c. Share in groups.

> The Gilded Age, which is the period following the American Civil War, was both a time of great prosperity and enormous poverty. The last three decades of the nineteenth century were the years in which American economy offered unparalleled opportunities to make great fortunes. Industrial magnates like Andrew Carnegie and John D. Rockefeller opened the way for corporate economy. **But this also set the scene for corruption and the ruin of a free-market economy.** Huge moguls had monopoly over the economy, and this resulted in the ruin of the small farmers who were unable to compete with the giant industrialists. This also meant that industrial workers and farmers had less economic and social security and were harshly exploited. Mark Twain, who coined the term in 1890, was a prominent figure who satirized the American society of the time. The term "gilded" indicated a society disguised in gold but with crudity and misery underneath the surface.

65. ACTIVITY–ARRANGE SENTENCES INTO A PARAGRAPH

a. The sentences below make up a paragraph. Arrange them in their logical order. Start with the topic sentence, and arrange the supporting sentences in a coherent manner.

- Ultimately, both Gatsby and Anderson's characters become disappointed and bitter upon discovering that the American Dream is an illusion.
- In "The Great Gatsby", published in 1925, the American Dream is supposed to represent independence and the opportunity to make one's fortune through hard work and perseverance.
- The American Dream has throughout times either represented selfish materialism or an ideal out of reach.
- However, it turns out to be just self-centered materialism and the pursuit of pleasure, in which excess and luxury prevail.
- In "The Egg", published in 1921, the family of the narrator works very hard and moves around in the country, setting up different kinds of businesses, in pursuit of material success.
- This is best illustrated by literary works such as "The Great Gatsby" by Scott Fitzgerald and "The Egg" by Sherwood Anderson.
- However, no matter how hard they try, the American Dream is out of reach, and the more they pursue it the more disillusioned they become.

b. Share in groups.

> The American Dream has throughout times either represented selfish materialism or an ideal out of reach. This is best illustrated by literary works such as "The Great Gatsby" by Scott Fitzgerald and "The Egg" by Sherwood Anderson. In "The Great Gatsby", published in 1925, the American Dream is supposed to represent independence and the opportunity to make one's fortune through hard work and perseverance. However, it turns out to be just self-centered materialism and the pursuit of pleasure, in which excess and luxury prevail. In "The Egg", published in 1921, the family of the narrator works very hard and moves around in the country, setting up different kinds of businesses in pursuit of material success. However, no matter how hard they try, the American Dream is out of reach, and the more they pursue it the more disillusioned they become. Ultimately, both Gatsby and Anderson's characters become disappointed and bitter upon discovering that the American Dream is an illusion.

66. ACTIVITY–FIND NOUNS, SYNONYMS AND AN UNRELATED SENTENCE

a. **Complete the following paragraph with the nouns in the box. Compare with a classmate.**

There are many (1) _____ to having a global language. To begin with, an international (2) _____ offers job (3) _____ worldwide. You also have the possibility to study at international institutions, such as universities or (4) _____. English is the official language of the United Nations, UNESCO, and most other international (5) _____. Moreover, English is the language you can use if you want to learn about the latest developments and (6) _____ within science and (7) _____. Another benefit offered by English as a common language is that you have access to international (8) _____, which updates you on what is going on around the (9) _____. What is more, a global language offers (10) _____ worldwide the opportunity to exchange experiences and opinions about various medicines and (11) _____. Lastly, English is important in international politics, as it facilitates (12) _____ about significant (13) _____ between countries.

> Issues, doctors, opportunities, treatments, media, advantages, language, technology, colleges, discoveries, organizations, world, communication

> 1. advantages 2. language 3. opportunities 4. colleges 5. organizations 6. discoveries 7. technology 8. media 9. world 10. doctors 11. treatments 12. communication 13. issues

b. **Find in the paragraph synonyms for the following words. Compare with a classmate.**

Globally, Chance, Crucial (3 words), Shared, Advancements, Findings, Simplify, Practices, Views, Problems, Collaborate

c. **Identify one sentence which breaks the unity of the paragraph. Underline it. Compare with a classmate.**

a.
1. advantages 2. language 3. opportunities 4. colleges 5. organizations 6. discoveries 7. technology 8. media 9. world 10. doctors 11. treatments 12. communication 13. issues

b.

globally	worldwide
chance	opportunity
crucial (3 words)	significant, important, essential
shared	common
advancements	developments
findings	discoveries
simplify	facilitate
practices	experiences
views	opinions
problems	issues
collaborate	cooperate
regularly	daily

67. ACTIVITY—ARRANGE SENTENCES INTO A PARAGRAPH

a. **Arrange the following supporting sentences into a coherent paragraph. The first and the last sentences have been provided.**

- By 1900, the United States became the world's leading industrial manufacturer.
- The United States industrialized speedily during the 1800s, ultimately exceeding Britain's dominance.
- Electricity was also essential for the spread of communication tools, such as the telephone and telegraph.
- Americans initiated various amazing technological inventions, such as the steamboat, the sewing machine, the tractor, and the typewriter.
- Besides, electricity would later be used in machines such as the motion picture projector and the computer.
- But the most important invention of the time was the use of electricity, which could be used for the operation of many devices both at home and in factories.

First sentence: *The beginning of American Industrial Revolution made the country gain industrial supremacy.*

Last sentence: *It was also in America that personal transportation became accessible to the general public due to Henry Ford's affordable automobile.*

b. **Share in groups.**

> The beginning of American Industrial Revolution made the country gain industrial supremacy. The United States industrialized speedily during the 1800s, ultimately exceeding Britain's dominance. By 1900, the United States became the world's leading industrial manufacturer. Americans initiated various amazing technological inventions, such as the steamboat, the sewing machine, the tractor, and the typewriter. But the most important invention of the time was the use of electricity, which could be used for the operation of many devices both at home and in factories. Electricity was also essential for the spread of communication tools, such as the telephone and telegraph. Besides, electricity would later be used in machines such as the motion picture projector and the computer. It was also in America that personal transportation became accessible to the general public due to Henry Ford's affordable automobile.

68. ACTIVITY–IDENTIFY LINKING WORDS

Identify all linking words in the following paragraph. Underline them. Compare with a classmate.

The Industrial Revolution brought about great changes in the way work was performed. Except for a few shopkeepers, nobody owned a clock in the early 1700s in the US. Work patterns were determined by nature and not the machines. Prior to industrialization, working the fields was a flexible activity, as one could always take a break at one's own discretion. Not to mention that there were no clocks or factory supervisors to keep track of time. Besides, most people could do different kinds of tasks and were not restricted to only one specialized job. Furthermore, working on a project from beginning to end, and seeing it as a finished product, was no longer part of the working process now. Shoemakers, weavers, and other craftsmen and craftswomen were incapable of competing with the pace and quantity of goods manufactured by factories. New railroads and factories made people change their pace of life too. Now they had to fit their actions to a timetable. This was experienced by many as deeply stressful.

69. ACTIVITY–IDENTIFY SYNONYMS AND THE TOPIC SENTENCE

a. **Find in the paragraph below synonyms for the words in the boxes.**

> Include, dominated, wealthy, accumulate, limited, crop, depended on, aid, scattered, thieves, vagabonds, unlimited, stances, menace, unwanted, housing, offer, unemployment, fit, separated

The population was rapidly increasing, and the social system was not flexible enough to fit them in its ranks. Business was monopolized by the privileged in society. There was no need of hands in farming either, which made an ever-increasing population to pile up in new towns and industrial areas. This resulted in a huge number of people outside a system which restricted their freedoms. Some of them worked on farms in the harvest seasons, but the rest relied on charity and public poor relief. Thousands of them spread through the country as beggars, robbers and prostitutes. What is more, the unrestricted growth of the population formed terrible attitudes of the rich towards the poor. Every child born in a workman's family was seen as a threat, a new unwelcome mouth to feed. The Poor Law of 1834 set up the workhouse system intended to provide shelter for the poor, sick and elderly. It was meant to offer food and clothing in exchange for work in times of joblessness. The Poor Law offered no cash support to those who were physically healthy and segregated the poor by sexes.

b. Choose a suitable topic sentence for the paragraph.

1. One of the consequences of the Industrial Revolution was the workhouse system.
2. There were a lot of poor people in the early 19th century Britain.
3. On the eve of the Industrial Revolution, economic conditions in Britain were very poor.

c. Share in groups.

a. **include**-fit **dominated**-monopolized; **wealthy**-privileged; **accumulate**-pile up; **limited**-restricted; **crop-harvest**; **depended on**-relied on; **aid**-relief; **scattered**-spread; **thieves**-robbers; **vagabonds**-beggars; **unlimited**-unrestricted; **stances**-attitudes; **menace**-threat; **unwanted**-unwelcome; **housing**-shelter; **offer**-provide; **unemployment**-joblessness; **fit**-healthy; **separated**-segregated;
b. On the eve of the Industrial Revolution, economic conditions in Britain were very poor.

70. ACTIVITY–IDENTIFY TOPIC SENTENCE AND LINKING WORDS

a. Study the following paragraph. Identify and underline linking words. Compare with a classmate.

Learning helps us adapt to our environment. In fact, it is vital for our survival. As societies become more complex, we need to adapt to new changes and challenges. But learning does not consist only of collecting knowledge, it entails change too. When we learn, we also change our behavior. Everything we learn is fluid and permanently shifting. Our knowledge becomes different from day to day and hour to hour. Our goals and interests do not stay static either. Interests "are but attitudes toward possible experiences", as John Dewey puts it. It depends both on the learner and the environment whether interests are pursued, and goals achieved. Furthermore, classroom learning is only a part of the learning process. For example, mathematical formulas offer an organization of logical knowledge and experiences. But while they serve as guides to future experiences and give direction, they are never the destination. The value of learning then is to get access to abstractions, classifications and generalizations that will help us create meaning out of future experiences.

b. **What is the main idea of this paragraph? Compare with a classmate.**

71. ACTIVITY–WRITE COMPLETE SENTENCES

a. **Answer the following questions in complete sentences.**

1. How do we learn from books?
2. How do we learn from experience?
3. How do we learn from other people?
4. How do we learn from the environment?
5. What is the best way to learn?

b. **Share in groups.**

72. ACTIVITY–WRITE A PARAGRAPH

Write a paragraph of at least six sentences which starts with the topic sentence suggested below.

We learn different things in different ways.

73. ACTIVITY–REWRITE A PARAGRAPH BY USING SYNONYMS

a. **Find in the paragraph below synonyms for the words in the box. Underline them. Compare with a classmate.**

> age, governed, productive, uneasiness, endless, conventional, establishments, called into question, produced, difficulties, strains, unquestionable, unparalleled, wide-ranging, aristocracy, immovable, contested

The period between the years 1837 and 1901 is known in the history of the United Kingdom as the Victorian era. It took its name from Queen Victoria who ruled the country during this time. It was one of the most prolific intellectual periods in the history of Britain and the world, but it was also a time of anxiety and continuous change. Traditional political, social, and religious institutions were questioned, changing Victorians' relationships to church, government, and social class. Indeed, the Industrial Revolution, with all its progress, generated new social problems, not to mention the emotional and intellectual demands on the individual. Even if all ages in history could be considered ages of change, it is undeniable that the Victorian age was without precedence. It represented a sweeping transformation from the past to the future. There was a departure from the rule of the church and the civil government ruled by the king and nobility. Besides, the fixed structure of the social classes in which rights and duties were clearly recognized and followed, were being challenged.

b. Go online and do research about the Victorian era. Use your research to write a paragraph with the topic sentence suggested below. (The focus of your paragraph should be *without precedence*.)

Even if all ages in history are considered ages of change, the Victorian age was without precedence.

74. ACTIVITY–COMPLETE A PARAGRAPH

Study the following paragraph and complete it with the right words from the box. Compare with a classmate.

> to keep up, much less, elevated, speed, quick, no hurry, contrast, faster, swiftly, fast

Many observers remarked that (1) _____ was one of the most striking characteristics of the last half of the nineteenth century. Victorians experienced both work and life happening extremely (2) _____. Industrial changes followed so (3) _____, that it was hard (4) _____ with the new realities of life. (5) _____ movement of people, goods, and communication increased the number of things one fitted in a day. This was in huge (6) _____ to what life looked like in the past, when people travelled (7) _____, were in (8) _____ to catch a train, and wrote occasionally a letter. Undoubtedly, the (9) _____ tempo of work and life was caused by an intellectual and mechanical boom too. Access to education contributed to the (10) _____ spread of knowledge, and consequently in the publication of books, newspapers, magazines, etc. This new way of life is described by the English novelist and poet George Eliot as the death of leisure.

> 1. speed; 2. fast; 3. swiftly; 4. to keep up; 5. Faster; 6. contrast; 7. much less; 8. no hurry; 9. elevated; 10. quick

76. ACTIVITY–ORGANIZE SENTENCES

The following sentences make up a paragraph. The topic sentence has been provided. Arrange the supporting sentences in a coherent manner.

- For her, not having money for a cup of tea is beyond imagination.
- When we identify ourselves with our social class, we risk narrowing our understanding of the world.
- Outside the shop, she is suddenly approached by a poor girl who asks her for "the price of a cup of tea."
- She does not feel pity nor compassion for the shabby girl, she is merely surprised and entertained by the strangeness of the situation.
- The rich view the poor as exotic and utterly different from everything they know.
- In Mansfield's short story "A Cup of Tea," Rosemary is a wealthy young woman finding herself deeply sad for not being able to buy an expensive enamel box in an antique shop.
- People outside our class become foreign creatures, who we rarely have empathy for.
- Katherine Mansfield illustrates how superior and distant the upper class can feel towards the lower class.
- Rosemary's immediate reaction, which seems so utterly strange, is "How extraordinary!"

When we identify ourselves with our social class, we risk narrowing our understanding of the world.

> When we identify ourselves with our social class, we risk narrowing our understanding of the world. People outside our class become foreign creatures, who we rarely have empathy for. Katherine Mansfield illustrates how superior and distant upper-class people can feel towards the lower-class. The rich view the poor as exotic and utterly different from everything they know. In Mansfield's short story "A Cup of Tea," Rosemary is a wealthy young woman finding herself deeply sad for not being able to buy an expensive enamel box in an antique shop. Outside the shop, she is suddenly approached by a poor girl who asks her for "the price of a cup of tea." Rosemary's immediate reaction, which seems so utterly strange, is "How extraordinary!" For her, not having money for a cup of tea is beyond imagination. She does not feel pity nor compassion for the shabby girl, she is merely surprised and entertained by the strangeness of the situation.

76. ACTIVITY–COMPLETE THE PARAGRAPH

a. Complete the paragraph below with the suitable words in the box. Compare with a classmate.

> bias, information, experience, preconceptions, status, competent, traditions, foreign, antipathetic, reactions, distinction, accept, power, negative

Everybody is familiar with the expression "do not judge a book by its cover", and yet we do it all the time. People have all kinds of (1) _____ about other people based on their appearances and not their character. Prejudice, also known as (2) _____, is a term used to indicate unfounded opinions we form of other people or groups of people. Prejudices are generally (3) _____ views formed on bits and pieces of (4) _____ we read or hear about, and which are not usually based on our personal (5) _____. We form prejudices about people based on their looks and (6) _____ in society. For instance, we tend to believe that beautiful people are smarter and more (7) _____ than others, that the rich are superior because of their money and (8) _____, and that some cultures are inferior in their customs and (9) _____. Very often, prejudices are unconscious emotional (10) _____ in our interactions with other people. We are, for example, fearful of people from cultures (11) _____ to us, and we are more accepting of familiar cultural values. In truth, biased attitudes are the results of the human need to make a (12) _____ between *us* and *them*. We find people who are different from us difficult to (13) _____, and thus pigeonhole them as (14) _____ or dangerous.

> 1. preconceptions; 2. bias; 3. negative; 4. information; 5. experience; 6. status; 7. competent; 8. power; 9. traditions; 10. reactions; 11. foreign; 12. distinction; 13. accept; 14. antipathetic

b. Discuss in groups.

1. What are prejudices?
2. What causes prejudices?
3. What are the consequences of prejudiced attitudes?

c. Write a paragraph.

Discuss some of the most common prejudices, their causes, and their effects on human relationships.

Suggested answer

Prejudiced behaviors are preconceived notions about people or groups of people. The most common prejudices are that religious people are intolerant, that the poor are ignorant, and that women are less intelligent than men. We form these prejudices from the stories communicated through media, the impressions we form from brief encounters, or from the opinions transmitted historically. Consequently, all religious people are labelled as extreme in their views, the poor are not given the opportunities they deserve, and women continue to be kept out of important spheres of life.

PARAGRAPH DEVELOPMENT– PARAPHRASING

We can develop a paragraph by paraphrasing other people's ideas and thoughts. To paraphrase - or rephrase - is to restate an idea or excerpt in your own words. When we paraphrase, the vocabulary is simpler and the structure of the sentence is modified. Besides, when we reword an author's sentences and ideas, we show that we understand them.

EXAMPLE OF PARAPHRASE

ORIGINAL TEXT	PARAPHRASED
"Man is an organism for reacting on impressions: his mind is there to help determine his reactions, and the purpose of his education is to make them numerous and perfect. Our education means, in short, little more than a mass of possibilities of reaction, acquired at home, at school, or in the training of affairs." William James, *Talks To Teachers On Psychology*	The purpose of education should not only teach us that there are many types of reactions in different situations of life. Education should also help us learn the best ways to react in various circumstances.
"Active, persistent, and careful consideration of any belief or supposed form of knowledge in the light of the grounds that support it, and the further conclusions to which it tends, constitutes reflective thought." John Dewey, *How We Think*	Reflective thinking involves active and careful reevaluation of our beliefs or knowledge based on new evidence.

77. ACTIVITY—WRITE A PARAGRAPH BY PARAPHRASING

a. English novelist and poet George Eliot describes in her novel "Adam Bede" the Victorian age as the death of leisure. Study the passage below from the novel.

Surely all other leisure is hurry compared with a sunny walk through the fields from "afternoon church", as such walks used to be in those old leisurely times, when the boat, gliding sleepily along the canal, was the newest locomotive wonder. Leisure is gone - gone where the spinning-wheels are gone, and the pack-horses, and the slow waggons, and the pedlars, who brought bargains to the door on sunny afternoons. Ingenious philosophers tell you, perhaps, that the great work of the steam-engine is to create leisure for mankind. Do not believe them: it only creates a vacuum for eager thought to rush in. Even idleness is eager now - eager for amusement; prone to excursion-trains, art museums, periodical literature, and exciting novels; prone even to scientific theorizing and cursory peeps through microscopes. Old Leisure was quite a different personage. He only read one newspaper and was free from that periodicity of sensations which we call post-time. He was a contemplative, rather stout gentleman, of excellent digestion. He was of quiet perceptions and undiseased by hypothesis, happy in his inability to know the causes of things, preferring the things themselves. He knew nothing of weekday services, had an easy, jolly conscience, and able to carry a great deal of beer or port-wine, not being made squeamish by doubts and qualms and lofty aspirations. Life was not a task to him, but a sinecure. Fine old Leisure!

b. Write a paragraph.

Paraphrase George Eliot's ideas. Use shorter sentences and synonyms. Focus on key words and phrases before writing your own sentences. Your paragraph should consist of about five sentences.

c. Share in groups.

Suggested answer

Gone are the days when a sunny walk from church required no other stimuli than the sun and the fields. Taking the boat and floating along the canal had no purpose but to enjoy tranquility. Do not be fooled to think that the steam-boat provides more leisure, it only creates room for eagerness. Everything has become eager now, even idleness itself. Everybody is keen on experiencing amusement and thrill. Excitement and sensationalism have become the mind's only cravings. Contemplation is gone, and so is the ability to enjoy things for what they are, instead of inspecting their causes.

78. ACTIVITY–VOCABULARY PRACTICE

a. Match the words on the left with their synonyms on the right. Compare with a classmate.

1. grow
2. haste
3. toil
4. repose
5. feverishly
6. reflect
7. adequate
8. deemed
9. scarcely
10. fatal
11. sap

1. restlessly
2. effort
3. think about
4. considered
5. barely
6. leisure
7. become
8. disastrous
9. impoverish
10. hustle
11. suitable

b. Match the words on the left with their antonyms on the right. Compare with a classmate.

1. salient
2. hurry
3. high pressure
4. locomotion
5. impatiently
6. rapidity
7. alone
8. adequate
9. habitually
10. sap
11. unsound

a. slowness
b. temperately
c. accompanied
d. insufficient
e. unimportant
f. infrequently
g. enrich
h. healthy
i. relaxation
j. rest
k. tardiness

Answer a
1. grow — a. become
2. haste — b. hustle
3. toil — c. effort
4. repose — d. leisure
5. feverishly — e. restlessly
6. reflect — f. think about
7. deemed — g. considered
8. scarcely — h. barely
9. adequate — i. suitable
10. fatal — j. disastrous
11. sap — k. impoverish

Answer b
1. salient — a. unimportant
2. hurry — b. slowness
3. high pressure — c. relaxation
4. locomotion — d. rest
5. impatiently — e. temperately
6. rapidity — f. tardiness
7. alone — g. accompanied
8. adequate — h. insufficient
9. habitually — i. infrequently
10. sap — j. enrich
11. unsound — k. healthy

79. ACTIVITY–REFLECT

a. Study the paragraph below from "Life at High Pressure" by William R Greg.

Beyond doubt, the most salient characteristic of life in this latter portion of the 19th century is its SPEED, what we may call its hurry, the rate at which we move, the high-pressure at which we work. We have got into a habit of valuing speed as speed, with little reference to the objects sought by rapid locomotion. We are growing feverishly impatient in temperament. Our love and pride in rapidity of movement, therefore, are under the circumstances natural enough, but they are not rational sentiments. A life without leisure and without pause - a life of *haste* - above all a life of excitement, such as haste inevitably involves – is a life filled so full, even if it is full of interest and toil, that we have no time to reflect where we have been and whither we intend to go. We have no time to reflect on what we have done and what we plan to do, still less what is the value, and the purpose, and *the price* of what we have seen, and done, and visited. This can scarcely be deemed an adequate or worthy life. We are, perhaps, most of us, conscious at some moments of our course of the need to be quiet, to be in repose, to be *alone*. But I believe few of us have ever estimated adequately the degree in which an *atmosphere of excitement*, especially when we enter it young and continue in it habitually, is fatal to the higher and deeper life. It saps solidity and strength of mind, and by slow and sure gradations, it carries us on towards a mental and moral condition which may justly be pronounced unsound.

b. Reflect and write complete sentences.

1. Describe *a hurried person*. Describe a person who values high activity and is impatient in temperament.
2. Describe *a hasty life*. Describe a life in which everything happens at high speed.
3. Name at least two things people who seek excitement and activity miss out.

c. Share in groups.

d. Write a paragraph of about seven or eight sentences that begins with the topic sentence suggested below.

A life of haste is a life of waste.

Suggested answer

b. 1. A hurried person is somebody eager to accomplish as much as possible, and who feels that time is of the essence. Besides, a hurried person is quick in thought and action, and becomes impatient when things take too long to do or get. 2. A hasty life is a very active life that consists of many activities and events. However, a hasty life lacks experiences in which the person lives in the moment. 3. People who live a hasty life miss out on the small things in life. They get restless in their free time, and need external stimuli to experience the thrill of the moment. They miss out on enjoying time with friends and family, and always seek novelty.

d. A life of haste is a life of waste. Of course, knows that we should stop and smell the roses as often as we can. There is no point in achieving things if we do not take time to enjoy them. But modern life encourages us to always do, consume and aspire for more. But haste only places us on a treadmill that never stops. If we fail to see life as a process rather than a destination, we fail to live it. Numerous studies show that when asked what they regret the most, people on their deathbeds have similar answers. They all regret having lived a life of haste, eager to accomplish things. Had they had the chance to go back, they would slow down and spend more time with the people around them. They would enjoy longer breaks and longer vacations. Ultimately, an unhurried life is a gratifying life.

80. ACTIVITY–WRITE A PARAGRAPH BY PARAPHRASING

a. **Study the following paragraph from the essay "Nobody is Home" by Charles Leadbeater.**

Home is where the heart is, and there is no place like home, yet a sense of being at home can come from many sources. Home can be a place of residence, where you go back to after work. It can mean the place you come from: where you grew up, and to which you return in your memories and for important family rituals. Feeling at home can come from an activity in which you feel at ease, in flow, in a landscape that's familiar and uplifting. Doing satisfying work can evoke a sense of home, as can being with friends or walking along a beach with someone you love. When the technology of the home was a place for the washing machine, the fridge, the boiler, the home was as a private, bounded space. Now technology is breaking down those boundaries. Young people seem to be most at home when they are on – or perhaps 'in' – their phones, flicking between apps, surfing their social networks.

b. **Rewrite this paragraph by using your own words and sentences. Begin your paragraph with the suggested topic sentence. Use at least three linking words.**

Home may mean a lot of things and can have many sources.

c. **Share with a classmate.**

> **Suggested answer**
>
> *Home may mean a lot of things and can have many sources. Home can be the place you return to after work. It can also be the place where you were born and grew up. Besides, home can be a place where you enjoy yourself, either by doing an activity or just being. In addition, doing a job that feels meaningful can be home. Similarly, being into a happy romantic or friendly relationship may feel like home. In contrast to the traditional home as a private space, today's technology breaks the privacy of home. Phones have become our home, but they are also means of transporting us beyond home boundaries.*

81. ACTIVITY–COMPLETE THE PARAGRAPH WITH EXAMPLES

a. Read the following half-finished paragraph, which lacks exemplifying sentences.

The short story "A Cup of Tea" by Katherine Mansfield teaches us several things about the life of the rich. To begin with, we learn that the rich cannot imagine what life without money looks like. Besides, they feel no empathy nor compassion for the poor. Instead, she lights a cigarette and orders brandy, expecting the girl to tell her an exotic story about her unfortunate life. Rosemary also reveals that despite their money, the wealthy can also lack self-confidence.

b. Read the following supporting sentences missing from the paragraph.

1. When she hears her husband describe Miss Smith very attractive, Rosemary suddenly feels insecure and hastily sends the girl home.
2. For example, when Rosemary is approached by the girl in the street, her reaction to the girl's complete lack of money is: "How extraordinary!"
3. For instance, when Rosemary takes the girl home, she does not offer her food straight away, or even try to understand how she feels.

c. Rewrite the paragraph by placing supporting sentences in their appropriate places.

d. Share with the class.

> The short story "A Cup of Tea" by Katherine Mansfield teaches us several things about the life of the rich. To begin with, we learn that the rich cannot imagine what life without money looks like. For example, when Rosemary is approached by the girl in the street, her reaction to her complete lack of money is: "How extraordinary!" Furthermore, they feel no empathy nor compassion for the poor. For instance, when Rosemary takes the girl home, she does not try to understand how she feels or offer her food immediately. Instead, she lights a cigarette and orders brandy, expecting the girl to tell her an exotic story about her unfortunate life. Besides, Rosemary reveals that despite their money, the wealthy can also lack self-confidence. When she hears her husband describe Miss Smith very attractive, Rosemary suddenly feels insecure and sends hastily the girl home.

NARRATIVE PARAGRAPHS

Narrative paragraphs tell a story. They present a series of happenings which focus around one main idea.

EXAMPLE

I was born in Tuckahoe, near Hillsborough, and about twelve miles from Easton, in Talbot county, Maryland. I have no accurate knowledge of my age, never having seen any authentic record containing it. By far the larger part of the slaves know as little of their ages as horses know of theirs, and it is the wish of most masters within my knowledge to keep their slaves thus ignorant. I do not remember to have ever met a slave who could tell of his birthday. They seldom come nearer to it than planting-time, harvest-time, cherry-time, spring-time, or fall-time. A want of information concerning my own was a source of unhappiness to me even during childhood. The white children could tell their ages. I could not tell why I ought to be deprived of the same privilege. I was not allowed to make any inquiries of my master concerning it. He deemed all such inquiries on the part of a slave improper and impertinent, and evidence of a restless spirit. The nearest estimate I can give makes me now between twenty-seven and twenty-eight years of age. I come to this, from hearing my master say, some time during 1835, I was about seventeen years old.

Frederick Douglass,
Narrative of the Life of Frederick Douglass, an American Slave

EXPLANATORY PARAGRAPHS

Explanatory paragraphs provide information about a certain subject. They are usually factual and contain research, but can also be based on the writer's knowledge.

EXAMPLE

We may ask how the child apprehends an orange out there on the table before him. It can not be said that the orange goes into the child's mind by any one of its senses. By sight he gets only the colour and shape of the orange, by smell he gets only its odour, by taste its sweetness, and by touch its smoothness, rotundity, etc. Furthermore, by none of these senses does he find out the individuality of the orange, or distinguish it from other things which involve the same or similar sensations - say an apple. It is easy to see that after each of the senses has sent in its report something more is necessary: the combining of them all together in the same place and at the same time, the bringing up of an appropriate name, and with that a sort of relating or distinguishing of this group of sensations from those of the apple. Only then can we say that the knowledge, "here is an orange," has been reached. Now this is the one typical way the mind has of acting, this combining of all the items or groups of items into ever larger and more fruitful combinations.

James Mark Baldwin, *The Story of the Mind*

82. ACTIVITY–IDENTIFY PARAGRAPH TYPE

a. **Study the following paragraph from the short story "The Egg" by Sherwood Anderson, and decide what type it is.**

My father was, I am sure, intended by nature to be a cheerful, kindly man. Until he was thirty-four years old, he worked as a farm-hand for a man named Thomas Butterworth, whose place lay near the town of Bidwell, Ohio. He had then a horse of his own and on Saturday evenings drove into town to spend a few hours in social intercourse with other farm-hands. In town, he drank several glasses of beer and stood about in Ben Head's saloon, crowded on Saturday evenings with visiting farm-hands. Songs were sung and glasses thumped on the bar. At ten o'clock father drove home along a lonely country road, made his horse comfortable for the night and himself went to bed, quite happy in his position in life. He had at that time no notion of trying to rise in the world. It was in the spring of his thirty-fifth year that father married my mother, then a country school-teacher, and in the following spring I came wriggling and crying into the world. Something happened to the two people. They became ambitious. The American passion for getting up in the world took possession of them.

b. What is the main idea of the paragraph?

c. Share with a classmate.

> a. It is a narrative paragraph. b. My father was a cheerful man before he met my mother and had me.

83. ACTIVITY–WRITE A PARAGRAPH

a. Write a narrative paragraph in which you recall a period in your life. Name some events, places, people, and what makes it memorable for you.

b. Share in groups or class.

84. ACTIVITY–IDENTIFY PARAGRAPH TYPE

a. Study the following paragraph from "Boredom: A Lively History" by Peter Toohey, and decide what type it is.

Boredom is a condition of the socialized and, for much of the time, of the well fed. There are of course exceptions – Andy Warhol was very skinny and he claimed that he was very bored indeed. But it is probably different for animals. The better fed they are, I suspect, the more liable they are to boredom. And it is no doubt true that dogs living with humans get more bored than dogs that live in the wild, perhaps because pet dogs don't need to spend so long foraging for food. They have more opportunity for boredom; more leisure, that is to say. It looks a little as if humans cause domesticated animals to feel boredom simply because they like them so much. It is also possible that lonely animals in captivity have a higher expectation of stimulation and if this is not addressed they become prone to boredom.

a. What is the main idea of the paragraph?

b. Share with a classmate.

> a. It is an explanatory paragraph. b. Boredom is a condition of the satisfied.

85. ACTIVITY - WRITE A PARAGRAPH

a. **Write a paragraph of at least five sentences which starts with the topic sentence below.**

Boredom visits us when life is easy.

b. **Share with the class.**

> **Suggested answer**
> Boredom visits us when life is easy. When all our needs are met, we feel comfortable. But comfort is also the result of familiar circumstances. And when our surroundings are well-known and predictable, they also become monotonous. There are no stimulations or elements of surprise anymore. As a result, we feel that time stands still. We feel that everything is deprived of meaning and excitement. What is familiar is stress-free, and therefore, boring.

86. ACTIVITY–REWRITE A PARAGRAPH BY USING SYNONYMS

a. **Find in the paragraph below synonyms for the words in the box. Compare with a classmate.**

> ennui, uninteresting, unsurprising, unavoidable, tedious, get away from, lengthy, lingering, aversion, similar, worthless, useless, associated with, incentive, unhappiness, introspective

There are two main forms of boredom, according to psychologists. A situation is boring when we feel that it is predictable and inescapable. As a result, we feel as if time stands still and we can look at ourselves from the outside. The first form of boredom, called simple boredom, is the result of monotonous circumstances that are difficult to escape. Typical examples of boring circumstances are long lectures, extended road trips, or prolonged dinners with uninteresting people. Disgust is, in fact, comparable to this form of boredom. The second form of boredom, called existential boredom, is the result of losing the sense of meaning. When we are existentially bored, we feel that things are meaningless, and life is pointless. Existential boredom is typically connected to a lack of desire or motivation to achieve something. Melancholy and depression are feelings closely associated with existential boredom. Existential boredom is largely experienced by very self-reflected individuals.

b. **Rewrite the paragraph by using synonyms.**

> ennui – boredom; uninteresting – boring; unsurprising – predictable; unavoidable – inescapable; tedious – monotonous; get away from – escape; lengthy – extended; lingering – prolonged; aversion – disgust; similar – comparable; worthless – meaningless; useless – pointless; associated with – connected to; incentive – motivation; unhappiness – depression; introspective – self-reflected

87. ACTIVITY–WRITE A PARAGRAPH

a. **Write a paragraph of at least five sentences which starts with the topic sentence below.**

   There are several things that I find extremely boring.

b. **Share in groups.**

> NB! In this task, you might want to use verbal nouns: <u>listening</u> to boring lectures, <u>waiting</u> in line for hours, <u>being</u> in the same room for days, <u>spending</u> time with the same people for weeks, etc. When *listening*, *waiting*, and *spending* have the properties of nouns, they take a singular form. *Listening to the same music over and over again is the most boring thing ever.*

> **Suggested answer**
> *There are several things that I find extremely boring. First of all, action movies that have very little dialogue and a lot of meaningless action bore me to death. Also, doing repetitive tasks which offer no intellectual challenge is a bore. Repetitive conversations with colorless people can be excruciatingly boring. For example, parties where people have superficial conversations make me really bored.*

COMPARISON PARAGRAPHS

Comparison paragraphs compare two persons or things by focusing on their *similarities* and/or *differences*, or contrast two persons or things by focusing only on their differences.

EXAMPLE ONE

Love is an art, and like any art, it needs practice to become great. First of all, discipline is crucial – nobody gets better at anything without a disciplined approach. Surely you can practice something just fine without any self-regulation, but it will be more like a hobby. However, self-mastery transforms your practice not only into becoming an expert in this art, it also provides you with a lifelong tool to overcome all kinds of challenges. Furthermore, no art is learned without patience – quick results do not belong with deep-seated learning. Being patient means you are committed to making the relationship meaningful both in the present and in the future. Ultimately, a great interest in art is a fundamental condition for its proficiency. Practicing love is truly about showing interest in and commitment to another person. You should be genuinely dedicated to and appreciate another human being.

EXAMPLE TWO

Respect is a far more valuable element of human relationships than love is. To begin with, love is an irrational feeling we cannot always explain, while respect is a rational opinion based on facts about a person. Furthermore, love is often based on a desire to own the person we love, whereas respect is given and earned without expecting anything in return. Respect involves a positive view of a person's actions, qualities and attitudes. We only offer and are offered respect regarding noble behavior. This is not the case with love, as we accept all kinds of attitudes and behaviors from the person we love. Indeed, love leaves us powerless in the face of unfairness and excess. Besides, respect is closely connected with wisdom and reliability, which we cannot say about love, as love is rarely wise. Finally, respect is something everybody can achieve if they want to, but love leaves us at the mercy of others – you either get it or not, and there is nothing you can do about it.

88. ACTIVITY—WRITE A COMPARISON PARAGRAPH

a. **In groups, make a list of three differences between reading a book and watching a film.**

b. **Write a comparison paragraph which starts with the topic sentence suggested below. Follow the writing frame recommended.**

Reading a book and watching a film are two different ways of experiencing a story.

First difference	Second difference	Third difference
Supporting sencence	Supporting sencence	Supporting sencence
Example to illustrate	Example to illustrate	Example to illustrate

Suggested answer

There are many differences between reading a book and watching a film. When we read a book, we use our imagination to picture the places and characters we read about. But when we watch a film, we receive immediate visuals of the setting and characters of the story. For example, when we read, we are free to imagine a character's looks and personality based on the words in the book. However, films do not give us this freedom, because they show actors and places that the director chooses for us. In addition, when we read a book, we need to think and pay attention to details. When we watch films, however, we are mostly passive and do not need concentration. Besides, watching a film allows us to do something else at the same time, such as eating or even exercising. Finally, watching a film can be a social activity, because you can watch a film with family or friends, or at the cinema. Reading a book, however, is mostly a lonely activity. People prefer to read a book alone because it helps them focus and understand it better. In conclusion, reading a book and watching a film are quite different experiences.

ARGUMENTATIVE PARAGRAPHS

One of the most important types of paragraphs are **argumentative paragraphs,** also called **opinion paragraphs**. This type of paragraph presents a personal evaluation of a certain issue by discussing its positive or negative aspects. It includes information, reasons, explanations, and exemplifications meant to convince the reader of the legitimacy of the view put forward.

EXAMPLE ONE
A global language such as English makes the world a better place for many reasons. To begin with, people across continents and nations are able to communicate and interact with each other. They can exchange opinions and perspectives about controversial topics, and ultimately come to a common understanding. When we grow up in a world where it is natural to hear, read and talk in a common language, we become more understanding and accepting of cultural differences. A universal language exposes people to different views and ways of life. Furthermore, people worldwide benefit from opportunities to study at international schools and universities, and thus use great resources of learning. English also makes research and technology accessible to all, something which enriches our lives. It offers better job opportunities worldwide, and expands people's professional prospects. Ultimately, English contributes to an interconnected world, making everybody feel part of a whole.

EXAMPLE TWO
One of the most fascinating psychological novels I have ever read is "Rebecca" by the English author Daphne du Maurier. Its storytelling is gripping and it transports the reader into a world that is never what it seems. First of all, it portrays the amazing transformation of the heroine from a naïve and insecure girl into a mature and wise woman. It also reveals people's prejudicial tendencies when they know little about each other. Generally, people form opinions of others based on their social status and prestige, and do not concern themselves with the truth. But most importantly, we learn that people's social standing and appearance place them automatically in the category of morally superior individuals. The truth is that they frequently turn out to be of a morally ambiguous nature, and only take advantage of people's naiveté and preconceptions. Ultimately, Daphne du Maurier offers us a lesson in how many of the opinions we hold of people are simply false and prejudicial.

89. ACTIVITY–VOCABULARY PRACTICE

a. **Match the words on the left with their synonyms on the right. Compare with a classmate.**

1. outrage		a.	courage
2. accusation		b.	assertively
3. hardship		c.	associated with
4. get away		d.	heatedly
5. connected to		e.	blame
6. enormous		f.	indignation
7. bravery		g.	meek
8. wrongdoer		h.	weakling
9. pushover		i.	implicate
10. involve		j.	huge
11. intensely		k.	pain-giver
12. exploiter		l.	snappish
13. humble		m.	adversity
14. forcefully		n.	escape
15. irritable		o.	profiteer

b. **Match the words on the left with their antonyms on the right. Compare with a classmate.**

1. stay around		a.	meek
2. useless		b.	attack
3. retreat		c.	furious
4. calm		d.	huge
5. tiny		e.	steer clear
6. confront			
7. cowardice		f.	assertively
8. a brave person		g.	unfair
9. just		h.	courage
10. subordination		i.	valuable
11. in a self-controlled manner		j.	heatedly
12. arrogant		k.	weakling
13. modestly		l.	escape
		m.	defiance

a.

outrage	indignation
accusation	blame
hardship	adversity
get away	escape
connected to	associated with
enormous	huge
bravery	courage
wrongdoer	pain-giver
pushover	weakling
involve	implicate
intensely	heatedly
exploiter	profiteer
humble	meek
forcefully	assertively
irritable	snappish

b.

stay around	escape
useless	valuable
retreat	attack
calm	furious
tiny	huge
confront	steer clear
cowardice	courage
brave person	weakling
just	unfair
subordination	defiance
in a self-controlled manner	heatedly

90. ACTIVITY–ARRANGE SENTENCES INTO A PARAGRAPH

a. Find two sentences which define anger in the sentences below.

- In truth, the profiteers of the earth are not the meek, but the assertively snappish.
- Anger is also associated with power that is used against unwanted behavior.
- Anger may have a beneficial role in the face of adversity.
- It helped the furious individual to get food before others did.
- It includes the element of blame and a feeling of personal offense.
- Besides, it is a huge advantage to put the pain-giver down than to steer clear.
- Furthermore, anger might be viewed as a sign of courage.
- An attack is more strategic than an attempt to escape.
- From an evolutionary perspective, anger has been valuable for survival.
- Whether we like it or not, worldly success generally implicates a degree of anger and defiance.
- Thus, anger can be a way of calling for respect.

- Undeniably, when one talks heatedly, people tend to stop and listen.
- Anger is a state of pain and is associated with annoyance, irritation and indignation.
- The individual who is incapable of anger in situations that seem unfair is sure to be seen as a weakling.

    b. **Find at least five recurrent (frequent) positive words (both adjectives and nouns) in the rest of the sentences.**

    c. **Find the topic sentence of the paragraph.**

    d. **Arrange supporting sentences in a logical manner. Rewrite the whole paragraph. (NB! In this paragraph, the topic sentence is the third sentence).**

    e. **Share in groups.**

---

a. Anger is a state of pain and is associated with annoyance, irritation and indignation. It includes the element of blame and a feeling of personal offense.

b. beneficial, strategic, power, valuable, advantage, respect, courage, success

c. Anger, generally seen as a negative emotion, may have a beneficial role in face of adversity.

d.
1. Anger is a state of pain and is associated with annoyance, irritation and indignation.
2. It includes the element of blame and a feeling of personal offense.
3. Anger may have a beneficial role in face of adversity.
4. Indeed, an attack is more strategic than an attempt to escape.
5. Anger is also associated with power, as it is used against unwanted behavior.
6. From an evolutionary perspective, anger has been valuable for survival.
7. It helped the furious individual to get food before others did.
8. Besides, it is a huge advantage to put the pain-giver down than to steer clear.
9. Thus, anger can be a way of calling for respect.
10. Furthermore, anger might be viewed as a sign of courage.
11. As a matter of fact, the individual who is incapable of anger in situations that seem unfair, is surely to be seen as a weakling.
12. Whether we like it or not, worldly success generally implicates a degree of anger and defiance.
13. Undeniably, when one talks heatedly, people usually stop and listen.
14. In truth, the profiteers of the earth are not the meek, but the assertively snappish.

91. ACTIVITY–USE LINKING WORDS

a. Complete the following paragraph with the appropriate linking words.

> In fact, Besides, It is not without reason, What is more, In contrast, Indeed, for instance, In addition, for example, To be clear

Anger is a self-destructive emotion. It often puts the angry individual at a disadvantage. (1) _____, an immersion in furious rage only makes a person rash in decisions and foolish in actions. (2) _____, anger presents itself as an unintelligent emotion because it disturbs reasonable thinking. (3) _____, it is easy to manipulate a furious individual because of his low level of mental discipline. (4) _____ that we admire those who show control over their emotional reactions. We admire their poised demeanor because we associate it with wisdom. (5) _____, anger is a transitory emotion, which reveals that the furious individual lacks anticipatory abilities. (6) _____, the wise person knows that by giving it time, fury diminishes. The Stoics, (7) _____, view anger as a vice and a sign of weakness. They also believe that anger shows the inability to bear temporary pain. (8) _____, anger reveals the incapacity to deal with other people's failings. Marcus Aurelius, (9) _____, advises us to reflect upon our own mistakes before getting angry with the wrongdoers. He also points out that meekness is a quality which makes us unconquerable. (10) _____, humbleness helps us develop immunity against the words and actions of others. For even the most malicious of people will not be able to hold on against us if we respond with humility and love.

b. What is the main idea of this paragraph?

c. Share with a classmate.

---

a. 1. To be clear 2. Besides 3. In fact 4. It is not without reason 5. What is more 6. In contrast 7. for example 8. In addition 9. for instance 10. Indeed.
b. People who give in to anger lack self-control and find themselves at a disadvantage.

92. ACTIVITY—WRITE A PARAGRAPH

a. **Discuss in groups.**

What are some *positive* aspects of anger? What are the *negative* effects of anger?

b. **Write an argumentative paragraph.**

Focus on both the positive and negative aspects of anger. Begin your paragraph with the topic sentence below. Remember to use linking words between sentences. Vary your vocabulary by using some of the words suggested. Your paragraph should be of about ten sentences.

There are both advantages and disadvantages to anger.

VOCABULARY BITES

ADVANTAGE, benefit, value, gain

DISADVANTAGE, downside, weakness, drawback

WRONGDOER, culprit, offender, guilty party

LINKING WORDS
On the one hand, on the other hand, to begin with, besides, in addition, however, yet, still, ultimately, finally

SYNONYMS FOR ANGRY
Annoyed, cross, irritated, indignant, furious, stormy

ANTONYMS FOR ANGRY
Calm, poised, collected, composed, self-possessed, levelheaded

SYNONYMS FOR ANGER
Fury, annoyance, indignation, rage, impatience, distemper

ANTONYMS FOR ANGER
Calmness, poise, self-possession, levelheadedness, even temper, cool head

Control, regulate, manage, balance
Give expression to, give free rein to, vent

Suggested answer

There are both advantages and disadvantages to anger. To begin with, anger is an indication that we have been treated unfairly. We want to the wrongdoing to be addressed. When we express anger, we also release the negativity from our system. Besides, anger can also call for respect and a change of attitude from others. Sometimes only anger can compel people to listen and correct their mistakes. However, anger has also many disadvantages. It shows lack of self-control and emotional weakness. It is the immediate reaction when we feel we have been wronged, and it takes a lot of mental effort to regulate our fury. But anger rarely solves the problem, and it is considered a weakness of character. Rage contrasts with calmness and poise which are qualities generally praised and highly valued.

93. ACTIVITY–USE NOUNS TO COMPLETE THE PARAGRAPH

a. Complete the following paragraph with suitable nouns. Share with a classmate.

> patience, perseverance, people, reality, partner, emotion, imperfections, songs, respect, imagination, person, control, love, education, responsibility

Many (1) _____ believe that love is something we accidentally bump into, and that only the blessed get to experience it, but I do not share that view. I believe that love is a product of (2) _____, and a subjective experience which distorts (3) _____. Besides, romantic (4) _____ is an emotion that does not last, it is only intense in the beginning, and it gradually fades when reality settles in. While all (5) _____, books, and movies tell us that love is perfect, reality is an imperfect affair. They deceive us into believing that there is a perfect (6) _____ out there for us: the one. This also makes us think that love is a passive (7) _____, for which there is no need to work but only enjoy. Yet, the truth is that love is a process of learning and (8) _____. In fact, the only love that lasts is the one involving (9) _____ and dedication. Love certainly involves accepting our partner's (10) _____ as part of who they are. What is more, love is taking (11) _____ by showing care and (12) _____. In truth, love makes us become a better (13) _____, for we want to be kindhearted for the one we love. Ultimately, love is not something accidental or out of our (14) _____. It involves hard work and (15) _____.

---

1. people 2. imagination 3. reality 4. love 5. songs 6. partner 7. emotion 8. education 9. patience 10. imperfections 11. responsibility 12. respect 13. person 14. control 15. perseverance.

b. Discuss in groups.

> ➢ Is love genuine if it needs work and perseverance?

94. ACTIVITY–VOCABULARY PRACTICE

a. **Match words with their definitions. Compare with a classmate.**

1. Leisure	a. a person who sells from door to door or in the street
2. Peddler[2]	b. the quality, state, or condition of being lazy or inactive
3. Bargain	c. a position requiring little or no work, an easy task or a child's play
4. Sinecure	
5. Vacuum	d. time free from work, when one can rest and enjoy hobbies
6. Idleness	e. an advantageous purchase, especially one acquired at less than the usual cost
	f. a space not filled or occupied, emptiness or void

b. **Match the words to the left with their synonyms to the right. Compare with a classmate.**

1. leisurely   a. somebody
2. sleepily   b. meditative
3. glide   c. lazily
4. ingenious   d. move smoothly
5. eager   e. clever
6. personage   f. impatient
7. contemplative   g. inclined
8. stout   h. brave
9. prone   i. laidback

c. **Identify words which are unrelated to the others in each set. Compare with a classmate.**

1. Rush in / move with urgent haste / eat moderately / deal with hurriedly
2. Periodical literature / weekly journals / travel agencies / quarterly magazines
3. Cursory peeps / hasty peeks / brief looks / TV series
4. Periodicity of sensation / regular exercise / regularity of excitement / episodic pleasure
5. Undiseased by hypothesis / unaffected by doubt / unchanged by disbelief / assured by success
6. Anxious times / jolly conscience / peaceful mind / happy mindset
7. Made squeamish by doubts / be dismayed by uncertainty / feel sick by hesitations / undisturbed by others' expectations
8. Lofty aspirations / biased attitudes / sky-high ambitions / soaring goals

---

[2] Pedlar – British English

a.
1. Leisure   a. time free from work, when one can rest and enjoy hobbies
2. Peddler   b. a person who sells from door to door or in the street
3. Bargain   c. an advantageous purchase, especially one acquired at less than the usual cost
4. Sinecure   d. a position requiring little or no work, especially one yielding profitable returns
5. Vacuum   e. a space not filled or occupied, emptiness or void
6. Idleness   f. the quality, state, or condition of being lazy or inactive

b.
1. leisurely   a. laidback
2. sleepily   b. lazily
3. glide   c. move smoothly
4. ingenious   d. clever
5. eager   e. impatient
6. personage   f. somebody
7. contemplative   g. meditative
8. stout   h. brave
9. prone   i. inclined

c.
eat moderately; travel agencies; regular exercise; assured by success; anxious times; undisturbed by others' expectations; biased attitudes

DESCRIBING VERSUS DISCUSSING

When we describe something, we tell how something *is*. When we discuss something, we tell how something *should be*. While the description of something is *a fact*, the discussion of something is *an opinion*.

When we express opinions in a paragraph, we also need to give good *reasons* for them. Every claim we make in a text must always be followed by supporting sentences in the form of information, explanations, examples, and ideas that support that claim. Besides, the tasks on tests and exams rarely involve describing things. As a rule, they require that you *discuss* different issues by offering your own interpretation and examination of a subject.

EXAMPLE	
DESCRIBING A GLOBAL LANGUAGE	**DISCUSSING A GLOBAL LANGUAGE**
A language is global when it is learned and spoken worldwide. It is not the language spoken by most people, but the language with the most geographical distribution, used in international organizations, as well as diplomatic, business, and academic relations across the globe. A global language functions as a lingua franca, which means it is the common language of communication among people of various linguistic backgrounds. English is the global language today, as it is the language of science, technology, media, trade, politics, etc. Besides, English is used in education, administration, and government as a means of communication between people of different languages. Moreover, English is part of the curriculum and learned as a main language in many schools worldwide. Even if English has spread across the globe with the expansion of the British Empire, today many versions of English emerge across the globe.	There are many advantages to having a global language. To begin with, an international language offers job opportunities worldwide. You also have the possibility to study and work at international institutions, such as universities or colleges. Moreover, English is the language you can use if you want to learn about the latest developments and discoveries within science and technology. Another benefit offered by English as a common language is that you have access to international media, which update you on what is going on around the world. What is more, a global language offers doctors worldwide the opportunity to exchange experiences and opinions about various medicines and treatments, with great benefits for patients all over the world. Besides, English is important in international politics, as it facilitates communication on significant issues between countries. Lastly, a common language is essential in matters of international security, essential for countries to cooperate daily in a globalized world.

95. ACTIVITY–STUDY PARAGRAPHS

a. Read the paragraphs below. Identify the main idea of each paragraph.

Paragraph 1

From medieval manuscripts to literature, many things contributed to transforming English into the global language it is today. The evolution of all languages has been influenced by history with a cultural importance for each country. I personally think that based on history and cultural values, the loss of national languages and cultures is impossible. During history, a lot of books and historical articles have been written in the local languages, which makes it difficult for people to allow English to affect their culture. Most ancient Latin texts are untranslated into English, which is proof that cultural heritage can't disappear. English as a global language has helped us to exchange cultural information and made us aware of the importance of the national languages. Besides, English has enriched our understanding of the world and made us value different cultures and languages. In addition, people's identity is strongly connected with their native language and the feeling of belonging to a certain culture. Meanwhile, English as a global language might slightly dissipate people's feeling of appreciation for other languages, and their importance in every culture. My conclusion is that English as a global language has a lot of advantages, but will not lead to any loss of national languages.

Paragraph 2

English may be the ruling language of the world, but we will always have national languages. While having one global language could be beneficial, the downsides to it are greater. The fewer languages people speak and understand, the less they are able to know about cultures that have existed throughout history. For example, literature that existed for centuries would be hard to interpret if we only had one language. Many historical texts were written in languages other than English, and translations are generally not accurate. If no one knows other languages beside English, how will we know what events took place before our time? Since language and culture often go hand in hand, the loss of a national language could also impact today's culture. The less we understand, the less knowledge we possess. Having a global language like English can be unifying, but the importance of protecting other languages is crucial. It's a good thing that we have a global language like English, but the world will always remain multilingual.

Paragraph 3

The loss of national languages and cultures is inevitable with English as a global language. This loss is happening right now. For example, in many non-English-speaking countries there are private schools where English is taught as a primary language. As a result, the culture is threatened because language is not just a collection of words and rules, it's part of a culture learned from an early age. English has taken over many words in other national languages, and people tend to use English words when they talk and write. I also use English instead of my native language sometimes, and many other people do the same. English is the official business language worldwide, as well as many other areas, such as the maritime, air navigation, and technology sectors. People are used to using notions and terminology easily available to them. This makes me believe that English as a global language is gradually causing the loss of national languages and cultures.

Paragraph 4

The loss of national languages and cultures becomes inevitable with English as a global language. This loss starts in the family, as parents encourage their children to use English as a primary language. In this way, they believe that their children will be more competitive in academic activities. Indeed, most textbooks are written in English. When you are good in sports, for example, speaking English is a great advantage when you compete internationally. Even socialization is much easier when one has a good command of English. Undeniably, everyone wants to sell themselves to the world and the best ticket to great opportunities is to master the global language. Another factor that contributes to the loss of local languages is that people travel as never before. When moving to a new country and finding opportunities for a good life, people can explore these opportunities better with a good command of English. They can have access to education, employment and friends and in this way, they settle in smoothly in their new country. This inevitably leads to the neglect of their native language.

Paragraph 5

The loss of national languages is inevitable with English as a global language. English language has spread to all parts of the world. In the past, it happened because of the UK and its power, but now it's happening because of the USA and its dominance in all aspects of human activity, especially in business and economy. Besides, the influence of popular American culture, like movies, TV programs, and music, is especially powerful among young people. Consequently, more and more English words entered everyday use and replaced the same words in the national languages. Furthermore, our world has become very global due to the internet, and it has made our lives much easier. For example, it facilitated communication with people around the world, it expanded online education, as well as business and trade. Because of all the above, it's important to have an international language. So, English as a global language opens the door to the world. However, people and their cultures are under attack, and, unfortunately, the loss of national languages and cultures happens slowly.

b. **Discuss in groups. Which of the tasks are these paragraphs based on?**

Task 1: *With English as a global language, the loss of national languages and cultures is imminent.*
Task 2: *English as a global language shows that there is no need for local languages and cultures anymore.*
Write an argumentative paragraph in which you discuss one of these statements.

c. **One of the paragraphs above describes more than discusses the statement of the task. Identify the paragraph and comment on what is missing.**

b. Task 1.

c. "Besides, the influence of popular American culture, like movies, TV programs, and music, is especially powerful among young people. Consequently, more and more English words entered everyday use and replaced same words of the national languages." These are the only sentences relevant in paragraph 5. The paragraph should be a discussion of whether national languages will disappear or not, and not a description. In other words, it should not describe the situation as it is today, but discuss with evidence and examples whether English will make local languages disappear.

96. ACTIVITY–DISCUSS THE FUTURE OF ENGLISH

    a. Go online and do research. Find out:

1. How many people speak English as a first language in the world today?
2. How many people speak English as a second language in the world today?
3. What are the top five most spoken languages in the world today?
4. Find at least one newspaper article in which *the future of English* is discussed: what are the main ideas of the article?

    b. Use your research findings as evidence to write an argumentative paragraph in which you discuss the future of English.

    c. Share with the class.

97. ACTIVITY–DESCRIBE WORK

    a. Answer the questions below by following the right sentence structure.

1. What is work?
2. What is physical work?
3. What is intellectual work?
4. What are some work values? (e.g. honesty, flexibility)
5. What is the relation between work and money?
6. What other types of work are there?

b. Share in groups.

c. Group sentences into a coherent paragraph in which you define and describe work. Use linking words.

Work is an activity which involves... Work can be divided into two main categories: ...

Suggested answer

a.

1. Work is an activity involving mental and physical effort made to achieve results.
2. Physical work involves using your body more than your brain, such as the jobs of a car mechanic, warehouse worker, or carpenter.
3. Intellectual or mental work involves using your brain rather than your body. Being a writer, scientist, and researcher involves doing intellectual work.
4. Some of the most important work values are flexibility, accuracy, honesty, and a respectable attitude. Being a good listener and a clear communicator are important at work. Punctuality, discipline, and dedication are also central values on a job.
5. Work is closely connected to money, it is in fact one of the main reasons why we work.
6. There is also work which does not involve money, such as domestic or voluntary work.

c.

Work is an activity involving mental and physical effort made to achieve results. Work can be divided into two major categories: physical work and intellectual work. Physical work, for instance, involves using your body more than your brain, such as the work of a car mechanic, warehouse worker, or carpenter. Intellectual or mental work, on the other hand, involves using your brain rather than your body. The work of a writer, scientist, or researcher, for example, is intellectual work. Some jobs, however, include both physical and mental work, as the job of a kindergarten assistant, nurse, or shopkeeper requires. Most of the time, money is the reason why we work. But there is also work which does not involve money, such as domestic or voluntary work.

98. ACTIVITY–DISCUSS WORK

a. Answer the questions below by following the right sentence structure.

1. Is work obligatory or optional?
2. Is work a right or a duty?
3. What is meaningful work?
4. What is meaningless work?
5. What is the relation between work and happiness?

b. Share in groups.

c. Group sentences into a coherent paragraph in which you discuss *why we work*. The topic and concluding sentences have been provided. Use linking words.

We work for various reasons.

Ultimately, work plays a great role in our lives, which shows how important it is to find the right vocation.

VOCABULARY BITES

Be employed as a researcher
Earn one's living as a part-time nurse
Work as a carpenter
Do the job of a secretary
Do house chores
Work as a volunteer, do voluntary work
To experience work as meaningful/meaningless
VERBS: Work, be employed, have a job, perform something, make efforts
NOUNS: Employment, job, position, occupation, profession, career

Suggested answer

a. 1. Work is for many people obligatory because people need to support themselves and/or their families. It would be impossible to have a decent life without the money we earn by doing work. 2. Work is both a right and a duty. It is a right because everybody should be given the chance to do what they are good at. It is also a duty because as members of a society, we need to contribute to its good functioning. 3. We experience work as meaningful when we feel we are good at it, and that we contribute to something bigger than ourselves. Besides, work feels meaningful when it matches our expertise and its tasks give us pleasure. 4. We experience work as meaningless when it does not match our skills and competence. Besides, a job can feel meaningless when we do not see the results of our efforts. 5. There is a close relation between work and happiness. In fact, if you are miserable at work, you cannot be happy when you return home at the end of the day.

c. We work for various reasons. To begin with, most people work to support themselves or their families. It would be impossible to have a decent life without the money we earn by doing some kind of work. Work is both a right people have to use their skills, but also a duty they have as members of a society. Everybody needs to contribute to the good functioning of their community. Besides, work and happiness are closely connected. If you are miserable at work, you cannot be happy when you return home at the end of the day. We are as a rule unhappy when we experience work as meaningless. This happens when our job does not match our skills and competence. A job can feel meaningless when we do not see the results of our efforts. Conversely, we experience work as meaningful when we feel we are good at it, and that we contribute to something bigger than ourselves. Ultimately, work plays a big role in our lives, and thus it is important to find the right vocation for ourselves.

99. ACTIVITY–REWRITE A PARAGRAPH BY USING SYNONYMS

a. Find in the paragraph below synonyms for the words in the box. Compare with a classmate.

> appraise, assert, components, remunerated, incorporate, gratuitous, charitable, related to, make amends, valued, happiness, suggest, elasticity, self-worth, achievement, support, accomplish, dignity, foundation

Work has been used to measure the good life since Plato. Many people claim that work and love are the most important elements of a healthy life. The simple definition of work is paid employment - 'to earn a living'. In the mid-1970s, it started to include also unpaid domestic work, as well as voluntary work. Work has often been associated with the religious view that it was forced on humankind to atone for past sins. In later years, however, work started to be appreciated as an important factor for human functioning and well-being. Some historians indicate that work improves our mental flexibility and self-esteem. Others found that being satisfied with the work we do offers us a sense of control and fulfilment. In fact, many historians declare work to be the pillar that gives structure to people's lives. Besides, through work, people achieve status and self-respect. It represents the basis of all human relationships.

> appraise – measure; assert – claim; components – elements; remunerated – paid; incorporate – include; gratuitous – unpaid; charitable – voluntary; related to – associated with; make amends – atone; valued – appreciated; happiness – wellbeing; suggest – indicate; elasticity – flexibility; self–worth – self-esteem; achievement – fulfilment; support – pillar; accomplish – achieve; dignity – self-respect; foundation – basis

b. Discuss in groups.

➢ How does work help us achieve self-respect?

100. ACTIVITY–DESCRIBE RESPONSIBILITY

a. Write complete sentences.

1. Describe a responsible person.
2. Describe a responsible parent.
3. Describe a responsible student.
4. Describe a responsible employee.
5. Describe a responsible citizen.
6. Does everybody have responsibilities?

b. Share in groups.

c. Group sentences into a coherent paragraph in which you define and describe responsibility. Use the topic sentence provided.

We all have responsibilities based on different roles we perform in society.

> RESPONSIBLE, *trustworthy, reliable, dependable, conscientious*
> RESPONSIBILITY, *obligation, duty, reliability, dependability*

Suggested answer

a. 1. A responsible person is someone who knows their duties and who assumes the consequences of their actions. Besides, a responsible person is somebody you can count on. 2. A responsible parent takes care of their children, and gives them love and protection. Responsible parents raise their children well, and listen and support them. Besides, they teach their children responsibility. 3. A responsible student comes on time, respects his/her teachers and classmates, attends classes, takes notes. He/she participates in class activities, does his/her homework, and prepares for tests and exams. 4. A responsible employee is punctual, knows and respects the rules of his/her workplace. Besides, a responsible worker respects and collaborates with his/her colleagues. 5. A responsible citizen obeys the law, votes in the elections, takes care of his/her surroundings and the environment, and pays taxes. 6. Everybody, as a member of a society, has duties and responsibilities. Living in a society means having all kinds of roles, such as a parent, or employee, or student. This means you interact with others and depend on them.

c. We all have responsibilities based on different roles we perform in society. Living in a society means having all kinds of roles, such as a parent, or employee, or student. For example, a responsible person is someone who knows their duties and who assumes the consequences of their actions. Besides, a responsible person is somebody you can count on. A responsible parent, for instance, takes care of their children, they give love and protection, raise them well, listen and support them. Besides, they teach their children responsibility. Similarly, a responsible student comes on time, respects his/her teacher and classmates, attends classes, takes notes and participates in class activities, does his/her homework, and prepares for tests and exams. In the same way, a responsible employee is punctual, and knows and respects the rules of his/her workplace. A responsible worker also respects and collaborates with his/her colleagues. A responsible citizen obeys the law, votes in the elections, takes care of his/her surroundings and the environment, and pays taxes.

101. ACTIVITY–DISCUSS RESPONSIBILITY

a. **Answer the questions below by following the right sentence structure.**

1. Why do we rely on responsible people?
2. Can intentions be more important than actions?
3. Should people be defined by their actions?
4. What are our responsibilities to others?
5. Are we more responsible for ourselves or for others?
6. How do we know where our responsibilities lie?

b. **Share in groups.**

c. **Group sentences into a coherent paragraph in which you discuss responsibilities we have to ourselves and others. Use the topic sentence provided.**

Topic sentence: *As moral beings, we constantly fulfil and benefit from different responsibilities.*

Suggested answer

a. 1. We rely on responsible people because we can trust them. Responsible people do what they must or promise to. Besides, they are supportive and caring. 2. It is difficult to know or appreciate somebody's intentions when they contradict their actions. Most often, actions are more important than words. Being responsible means that you think well before doing something. However, if you fail to do that, you must be prepared to take responsibility for your mistakes. 3. People are imperfect and many times they do stupid things which they regret. Our actions do not always tell the true story. We tend to learn from our mistakes, but most often what is done is done. The only thing we can change is our future behavior. That is why we should not always judge people based on their past actions. 4. We should always show respect to other people. It is our responsibility to try to understand and care for others. Besides, we are responsible to help others in need whenever we can. 5. It is natural to feel that we are primarily responsible for ourselves. We should take care of our health and wellbeing, and look after the people close to us. However, being responsible for ourselves does not need to be in contradiction with being responsible for others too. Yet, it is human to fight for self-preservation first and foremost 6. Social life involves a lot of rules which we learn from an early age. First, we learn our responsibilities from our parents, then from our teachers and friends, and later from our life in society in general. Besides, every country has laws and rules that its citizens must know, and conduct themselves in accordance with them.

c. As moral beings, we constantly fulfil and benefit from different responsibilities. Being responsible means you know that actions, and not intentions, count the most. You must be prepared to take responsibility for your mistakes. People are imperfect and many times they do irresponsible things which they regret. Yet, our actions do not always tell the true story. In fact, we tend to learn from our mistakes, but what is done cannot be undone. The only choice we have is to change future behavior. That is why we should not always judge people based on their past actions. Besides, we should always show respect to other people, because it is our responsibility to try to understand and care for others. We should also take care of our health and wellbeing, and look after the people close to us. However, being responsible for ourselves does not mean we are not responsible for others too. Ultimately, social life involves a lot of rules which we learn from when we are young. First, we learn our responsibilities from our parents, then from our teachers, and later from our life in society in general. Finally, as citizens of a country, we must conduct ourselves according to its laws and rules.

---

102. ACTIVITY–COMPLETE A PARAGRAPH

a. **Study the following paragraph. The sentences in the box below are missing. Set them in their appropriate place in the paragraph.**

Social responsibility is one of the most important issues people need to deal with today. Many people feel fear and anxiety about the future. We all fulfil certain roles in society, such as the roles of parents, teachers, nurses, friends, etc. But how do we make the duties of these roles compatible with the duties of citizens and inhabitants of the world? How do we reconcile our personal values with universal values? Second, it is our responsibility as human beings to accept people's differences and realize that individual values are not general values. Hence, we need to take care of ourselves and others if we want to live a satisfying life. Self-preservation is fundamental to human nature, and we tend to act in self-interest most of the time. But it is to our advantage to value the interests of others.

> - Social, economic, and environmental challenges are all around us, and it is our individual and collective responsibility to tackle them.
> - First, it is our duty as reasonable beings take responsibility for our environment.
> - Besides, no man is an island, we live together with other people.
> - Looking out for our fellow men and women is a wise long-term strategy for a good life.

b. **Compare with a classmate.**

> Social responsibility is one of the most important issues people need to deal with today. Many people feel fear and anxiety about the future. **Social, economic, and environmental challenges are all around us, and it is our individual and collective responsibility to tackle them.** We all fulfil certain roles in society, such as the roles of parents, teachers, nurses, friends, etc. But how do we make the duties of these roles compatible with the duties of citizens and inhabitants of the world? How do we reconcile our personal values with universal values? **First, it is our duty as reasonable beings take responsibility for our environment.** Second, it is our responsibility as human beings to accept people's differences and realize that individual values are not general values. **Besides, no man is an island, we live together with other people.** So, we need to take care of ourselves and others if we want to live a satisfying life. Self-preservation is fundamental to human nature, and we tend to act in self-interest most of the time. But it is to our advantage to value the interests of others. Looking out for our fellow men and women is a wise long-term strategy for a good life.

103. ACTIVITY–DESCRIBE MOTIVATION

a. **Answer the questions below by following the right sentence structure.**

1. What is motivation?
2. What is a motivated learner?
3. What is a motivated teacher?
4. What is a motivated employee?
5. What do you enjoy doing?
6. What is the link between motivation and rewards?

b. **Share in groups.**

c. **Group sentences into a coherent paragraph in which you define and describe motivation. Use the linking words provided.**

Motivation is the willingness to…

Suggested answer

a. 1. Motivation is the willingness and enthusiasm to do something. It is usually a goal-oriented activity based on the pleasure of its rewards. 2. A motivated learner is a person eager to learn and to use the knowledge for later projects. Motivated learners study a lot, attend classes, take notes and prepare diligently for tests and exams. 3. A motivated teacher is interested in his/her job and gives a lot of effort and time to their students. Besides, motivated teachers are dedicated and curious, and seek to improve their competence all the time. 4. A motivated employee is dedicated to his/her job. Motivated employees feel appreciated and perform their jobs in the most effective ways. They enjoy what they do, and are willing to learn to improve their skills and competence. 5. I enjoy doing the things I feel I am good at. I enjoy reading and writing and this also motivates me to become better at it. I believe that feeling competent and appreciated are the greatest factors of motivation. 6. We usually feel motivated to do the things we know will end in some sort of payoff. Most motivated behaviors are based on expected rewards.

c. Motivation is the willingness and enthusiasm to do something. It is usually a goal-oriented activity based on the pleasure of its rewards. For example, a motivated learner is a person eager to learn. Motivated learners study a lot, attend classes, and prepare for tests and exams. A motivated teacher, for instance, is interested in his/her job and gives a lot of effort and time to his/her students. Similarly, a motivated employee is dedicated to his/her job. Motivated employees feel appreciated and perform their jobs effectively. We generally feel motivated to make efforts when we expect some form of payoff in the future.

104. ACTIVITY–DISCUSS MOTIVATION

a. **Answer the questions below by following the right sentence structure.**

1. How are children motivated by their parents?
2. How are students motivated by their teachers?
3. How are employees motivated by their employers?
4. How are we motivated by our needs?
5. How are we motivated by our culture?
6. How do our dreams motivate us?

b. **Share in groups.**

c. **Group sentences into a coherent paragraph in which you discuss how we are motivated by things and people. The paragraph should begin with the topic sentence provided.**

We are motivated by different things and people in various ways.

Suggested answer

a. 1. Parents are the most important source of motivation for their children. They are role models for their children, they explain why things are done, and how and why they should be done. 2. Students are motivated by teachers who can see them and what they are good at, and who encourage and help them to become even better. 3. Employees are motivated by employers who appreciate their work, and who are interested in the workers' wellbeing. 4. We are motivated first and foremost by our needs. For example, the need for financial security motivates us to get an education and then a job that will offer us economic comfort. 5. In competitive societies, people are motivated to work hard and achieve successful careers. In collectivistic societies, people are less motivated by material success and are inspired to lead a more spiritual life. 6. Dreams, just like our needs, influence our behavior, and represent the things we want to have in life. They keep us going and guide our efforts.

c. We are motivated by different things and people in various ways. Parents are the most important source of motivation for their children. Teachers are a source of motivation for their students, as they support and encourage them in their learning. Workers are motivated by employers who appreciate their work, and who are interested in the workers' wellbeing. Most importantly, though, we are motivated by our needs. For example, the need for financial security motivates us to get an education and then a job that will offer us economic comfort. When we need emotional security, we are motivated to create relationships that will provide us with heart-warming feelings. Besides, every culture has its own incentives to certain behaviors. In some competitive societies, for instance, people are motivated to work hard and achieve successful careers. In less competitive societies, however, people are motivated to enjoy the little things in life, and are less motivated by material success. Ultimately, our dreams are a strong motivator of our behaviors, as they inspire us to keep going and remind us that our efforts have a purpose.

---

105. ACTIVITY—USE LINKING WORDS

Complete the following paragraph with suitable linking words. Compare with a classmate.

> ultimately, indeed, in fact, but, for example, in the same way, for instance, similarly, yet, what is more

Motivation is one of the most important elements of human behavior. (1) _____, everything we do in our everyday life, such as learning and achieving at school, in sport, in the kitchen, at work, etc. are intended, goal-oriented behaviors. There are two major types of motivation behind our activities: intrinsic and extrinsic motivation. Intrinsic motivation refers to the things we do for ourselves because we find them interesting or meaningful. Extrinsic motivation refers to the future rewards that come with doing certain things. (2) _____, these two types are not always different. (3) _____, they overlap most of the time. Motivation is a process, and not a result, and it can be observed in the person's choice of tasks, perseverance, effort, and speech. A motivated behavior is determined by goals, and most studies about motivation focus on how people deal with difficulties and failures while pursuing their goals. (4) _____ what motivates people the most is the element of usefulness and feeling of growth that they experience when they perform tasks. Performing well or performing better than others is a motivating factor for sustaining such activity. (5) _____, human needs determine the motives behind our acts. (6) _____, we are motivated by our hunger to search for food. (7) _____, we are motivated by exhaustion to seek our beds and go to sleep. The need for affection, (8) _____, motivates us to create relationships with other people. (9)

_____, the need for financial security makes us get an education and find a good job to achieve that. (10) _____, motivation is the foundation of all human endeavors.

> 1. Indeed 2. Yet 3. In fact 4. But 5. What is more 6. For example 7. In the same way 8. for instance 9. Similarly 10. Ultimately

106. ACTIVITY–IDENTIFY TOPIC SENTENCE

a. **Study the following paragraph. Identify and underline its topic sentence (*hint: it is not the first sentence!*).**

We can only see with our eyes and hear with our ears, this is truly the purpose of these organs. For example, a knife is designed to cut things. We can, of course, use other tools to cut something, but it would not be as clean and efficient. A knife is specifically made to cut things and it is what it does best. Thus, we can say that each thing has an end and a special quality. When deprived of that quality or when having a defect, it cannot fulfill its end properly. Just like eyes and ears are the ends of themselves - to help us see and hear - the aim of the soul is to be happy, Socrates tells us. According to him, we cannot live a happy life if we do not fulfill our best quality. Happiness means doing what we are meant to do best. Aristotle believes that the merit of all human beings is in their work. It is through work that one can be good and have a satisfying life. Every person has some special ability, and it is one's duty to reason, find what that ability is and use it. A carpenter's work, for instance, is to build materials for the construction of a building, and if he/she does it well, this is his reward. A nurse finds happiness in caring for the sick and, and she/he finds happiness in doing the job well. By doing their work well, people create a harmonious relationship between their personal and social self. They feel that they contribute to the wellbeing of their community.

b. **What is the main idea of this paragraph?**

c. **Share with the class.**

> Main idea: We all excel at something and we find happiness when we do what we are good at.
> Topic sentence: Happiness then means doing what we are meant to do best.

107. ACTIVITY–WRITE ABOUT YOURSELF

a. **Write an argumentative paragraph of at least ten sentences in which you discuss *one thing that you are very good at*.**

Focus on the following aspects:

1. Name one skill or aptitude you have: *Describe the skill in general.*
2. Discuss your evidence: *How have you discovered your skill?*
3. Why is it important to be good at something? *Is there a connection between mastery and happiness?*

b. Share in groups.

> # WRITING ARGUMENTATIVE PARAPGRAPHS
>
> To persuade, which means to convince and influence somebody of something, is part of everyday life. We do it all the time, as we regularly express opinions and interpretations of different issues. When we write, the moment we make a claim or a statement, we have to offer our reasons for why we believe that. In English, both persuasive and argumentative terms are used to indicate opinion pieces or texts.

108. ACTIVITY–ONLINE OR OFFLINE COMMUNICATION

An ideal communication, roughly defined as an exchange of information, is a well-balanced combination of online and offline interaction between people. However, in order to make your writing process stimulating, you will have to choose one type of communication to defend in a paragraph. In this way, you will need to expand on the implications of online and offline communication, and give good reasons for your choice. It is important to include examples in your paragraph.

a. Read the definitions of the two concepts.

Online communication – contact or interaction via e-mail, instant messaging (such as Skype or Messenger), contact forms on blogs and web-sites, forums, and other social networks (such as Instagram or Twitter). This type of communication involves writing short messages, sending documents, pictures, audio files, as well as emoticons that show feelings and emotions the person experiences at the moment.

Offline communication – contact or interaction face to face in a room or physical place, in which people can see and hear each other. In this type of communication, people use their bodies to speak, smile, look, make gestures, as well as listen and nod. They express their thoughts in their speech, and show positive emotions in their body language, such as by smiling or laughing, and negative emotions by frowning or crying.

   b. **Answer the following questions in complete sentences.**

   1. What would you be able to live without: offline or online communication?
   2. Which is more rewarding?
   3. Which is more honest?
   4. Which is more inclusive?
   5. Which is more restrictive?

   c. **Share in groups.**

   d. **Write a paragraph.**

Argue either for online or offline communication. It is important to choose one of them and defend its superiority. Your paragraph should be of at least ten sentences. Make sure you begin the paragraph with a topic sentence. All other sentences should be supporting sentences of the topic sentence. Include linking words.

109. ACTIVITY–PERSONAL OR PROFESSIONAL FULFILLMENT

An ideal life is one in which we experience both personal and professional fulfillment. However, in order to make your writing process stimulating, you will have to choose one type of success to defend in a paragraph. In this way, you will need to expand on the implications of personal and professional success, and give good reasons for your choice. It is important to include examples in your paragraph.

   a. **Read the definitions of the two concepts.**

Personal fulfillment is usually defined in terms of satisfying relationships, such a happy family and good friends. One achieves personal fulfillment by establishing a family and making permanent reliable friendships. Personal fulfillment is also experienced as a rather spiritual accomplishment, it is not measured in social prestige, but in social meaningful encounters.

Professional fulfillment is usually defined in terms of a fulfilling career, such as a prestigious job that pays well. One feels professionally fulfilled by performing well at work, and thus gain financial rewards and acknowledgments. Professional fulfillment is also experienced as a matter of social prestige, in which one is appreciated for the position one holds and the job one does.

b. Answer the following questions in complete sentences.

1. What would you be able to live without: personal or professional fulfillment?
2. Which is more nourishing?
3. Which is more permanent?
4. Which offers more freedom?
5. Which offers more self-satisfaction?
6. Which offers more self-doubt?

c. Share in groups.

d. Write a paragraph.

Argue either for personal or professional fulfillment. It is important to choose one of them and defend its superiority. Your paragraph should be of at least ten sentences. Make sure you begin the paragraph with a topic sentence. All other sentences should be supporting sentences of the topic sentence. Include linking words.

110. ACTIVITY–JACK OF ALL TRADES OR EXPERT

What is the best approach to competence? To know a little of everything or to be an expert in a very specialized field? You have to choose one type of skillfulness to defend in a paragraph. In this way, you will need to expand on the implications of being *good at a lot of things* or *great at one thing*. Choose one of them and defend it in a paragraph. It is important to give good reasons for your choice and include examples.

a. Read the definitions of the two concepts.

Jack of all trades and master of none is an expression used to describe a person who can do different kinds of work, but who is not great at any of them. A person good at many things knows a little from various, often unrelated, fields, such as arts, mathematics, biology and literature, etc., but does not have knowledge beyond a superficial level.

An expert is a person with deep knowledge and expertise within a specific field, such as evolutionary psychology, or railway engineering, etc. An expert's competence is limited to their field of activity, with very little or no knowledge from other fields. However, the proficiency of an expert is profound and comprehensive, making her/him reliable and a source for others to turn to for consultation.

b. Answer the following questions in complete sentences.

1. Which is more useful?
2. Which offers more motivation?

3. Which offers more satisfaction?
4. Which offers more creativity?
5. Which is more rewarding?

   c. **Share in groups.**

   d. **Write a paragraph.**

Argue either for being good at many things or expert in one. It is important to choose one of them and defend its superiority. Your paragraph should be of at least ten sentences. Make sure you begin the paragraph with a topic sentence. All other sentences should be supporting sentences of the topic sentence. Include linking words.

WRITING REFLECTIVE PARAGRAPHS

Reflection and critical thinking are crucial skills in life. By contemplating the impressions and feelings of our experiences, we create a meaningful relationship with our understanding of the world. Writing offers us the opportunity for a clear and more organized exploration of how we understand others' opinions and their relation to our own views. Besides, when we write, we explore an invaluable opportunity to gain self-knowledge and to learn how to communicate our thoughts coherently. Ultimately, beside bolstering our writing skills, reflective writing helps us explore our own learning and create meaning out of it.

III.   ACTIVITY–REFLECT OVER RESPONSIBILITY

   a. **Read the text below.**

In one of Katherine Mansfield's short stories, "The Garden Party", the concept of responsibility emerges when a man dies in the cottages close to the Sheridans' house. The Sheridans are an upper-class family planning a garden party on the same day they find out about a dead man in the cottages close by. He left a wife and six children behind. Laura, one of the young ladies in the family, immediately assumes that the party will be cancelled, but this is not an opinion shared by the rest of the family. Both Laura's mother and her sister Jose become angry with Laura when she insists on stopping the party. Laura believes that it is the right thing to do, and that going on with the plans would be very unkind. It is, however, not hard to convince Laura that having the party is just how things should happen. In truth, she wants to have the party, she has been looking forward to it for days. We see Laura torn between her deep desire to have the party and the feeling of guilt and responsibility for the family who is mourning close by.

b. Answer the following questions in complete sentences.

1. How responsible are we for other people?
2. Is it right to enjoy ourselves when strangers are suffering?
3. Does our personal happiness have anything to do with the happiness of others?

c. Share with the class.

d. Write a paragraph that begins with *one* of the two topic sentences below.

It is immoral to enjoy yourself when you are aware of somebody suffering at the same time.

If we let other people's suffering affect our own happiness, we can never be happy.

112. ACTIVITY–REFLECT OVER TRAVEL

a. Read the text below.

G. K. Chesterton declares in "What I Saw in America" that travel, instead of broadening the mind, narrows it. The writer believes that we feel a human bond with all humanity when we are at home, since "that is not an illusion. On the contrary, it is rather an inner reality. In a real sense any man may be inside any men. But to travel is to leave the inside and draw dangerously near the outside." When we are at home, we think about different cultures and customs as exotic and interesting, even if strange and far away. However, when people travel, they are obliged to face and experience those cultural differences. "Many modern internationalists talk as if men of different nationalities had only to meet and mix and understand each other. In reality that is the moment of supreme danger—the moment when they meet," the English writer declares.

b. Answer the following questions in complete sentences.

1. Are people more alike or more different than we think?
2. Why is it easier to be tolerant with people when they live away from us?
3. Do you agree with Chesterton that travel narrows the mind?
4. When does travel educate the mind?

c. Share with the class.

d. **Write a paragraph that begins with the topic sentence below.**

Travel, just like any experience, can be educative on several conditions.

113. ACTIVITY–REFLECT OVER LEARNING

a. **Study the following text.**

John Lubbock declares in "The Pleasures of Life" that the great mistake of education is to confuse instruction with education. Many learning activities exercise the memory rather than cultivate the mind. Children "are oppressed by columns of dates, by lists of kings and places, which convey no definite idea to their minds, and have no near relation to their daily wants and occupations." The English politician tells us that we should, in fact, do the opposite, we should give learners a "variety of mental food, and endeavor to cultivate their tastes, rather than to fill their minds with dry facts. The important thing is not so much that every child should be taught, as that every child should be given the wish to learn." The quantity of knowledge acquired in school today does not generally correspond to a thirst of learning outside school and later in life. Lubbock suggests that learners should be "trained to observe and to think, for in that way there would be opened out to them a source of the purest enjoyment for leisure hours, and the wisest judgment in the work of life."

b. **Answer the following questions in complete sentences.**

1. What do you think mental food is?
2. What do you think dry facts are?
3. What causes a thirst for learning?
4. What is the difference between a teacher who instructs and a teacher who guides?
5. How does education help us enjoy our leisure?

c. **Share with the class.**

d. **Write a paragraph in which you comment on the following idea:**

The important thing is not so much that every child should be taught, as that every child should be given the wish to learn.

114. ACTIVITY–REFLECT OVER IMAGINATION

a. Study the following text.

Arthur Christopher Benson expresses in "The Training of the Imagination" his surprise at the lack of focus on imagination in education, as he believes that imagination, just like any other faculty, should be trained. Imagination has a huge influence on our capacity to process past and predict future experiences. But most importantly, "the faculty of imagination plays an immense part in all human happiness and unhappiness, considering that, whenever we take refuge from the present in memories or in anticipations, we are using it." The truth is that imagination is one of the most powerful instinctive forces of the mind, and it is puzzling that education pays so little attention to how important it is to train and develop it. Imagination offers us the luxury of privacy and it lets us block out our surroundings. Without doubt, it is the learner's means of escape from tedious tasks and lectures. As the English essayist puts it, "probably the greater part of a human being's unoccupied hours, and probably a considerable part of the hours supposed to be occupied, are spent in some similar exercise of the imagination." Thus, training the imagination is crucial, as it helps us to ponder over everything that happened and everything that might happen to us in a sensible manner.

b. Answer the following questions in complete sentences.

1. How does imagination help us remove ourselves from tedious situations?
2. What are the advantages and disadvantages of recalling past memories?
3. What are the advantages and disadvantages of anticipating future events?
4. Do you agree with Benson's claim that imagination should be trained and carefully examined?

c. Share with the class.

d. Write a paragraph in which you comment on the quote below.

"It is no exaggeration to say that the greater part of human happiness and unhappiness consists in the dwelling upon what has been, what may be, what might be, and, alas, in our worst moments, upon what might have been."

115. ACTIVITY–REFLECT OVER EDUCATION AND VALUES

a. Study the following paragraph taken from "The Training of the Reason" by W.R. Inge.

The ideal object of education is that we should learn all that it concerns us to know, in order that thereby we may become all that it concerns us to be. In other words, the aim of education is the knowledge not of facts but of values. Values are facts apprehended in their relation to each other, and to ourselves. The wise man is he who knows the relative values of things. In this knowledge, and in the use made of it, is summed up the whole conduct of life. What are the things which are best worth winning for their own sakes, and what price must I pay to win them? And what are the things which, since I cannot have everything, I must be content to let go? How can I best choose among the various subjects of human interest, and the various objects of human endeavour, so that my activities may help and not hinder each other, and that my life may have a unity, or at least a centre round which my subordinate activities may be grouped. These are the chief questions which a man would ask, who desired to plan his life on rational principles, and whom circumstances allowed to choose his occupation. He would desire to know himself, and to know the world, in order to give and receive the best value for his sojourn in it.

b. Answer the following questions in complete sentences.

1. What do you think you should know so that you can become what you should be?
2. What are the most important values which represent the life you want to live?
3. What do you think Inge means when he declares that a wise person knows the relative values of things?
4. Which things are you prepared to let go and which things are you prepared to strive for?

c. Share in groups.

d. Write a paragraph in which you comment on the statement below.

Education helps us to sort out the right values for our life, and thus guides us in choosing the appropriate activities to dedicate ourselves to.

CHAPTER 3–ESSAYS

In this chapter, you will learn about:

- ✓ *the elements and structure of an essay*
- ✓ *two main kinds of essays: argumentative and comparison*
- ✓ *how to cite evidence in your essay*
- ✓ *how to read a task*
- ✓ *practice writing argumentative and comparison essays*

THE ESSAY

An essay is a coherent set of ideas organized into paragraphs that focus on one central argument or point of view. Every essay is divided into three parts: a beginning – the *introduction*, a middle – *body paragraphs*, and an end – the *conclusion*. Both the introduction and the conclusion have fixed positions in the essay and consist of one paragraph each. The middle of the essay comprises at least two middle paragraphs. An adequate essay rarely requires more than three body paragraphs.

While essays can be divided into several types, we are going to focus on two kinds: *argumentative*, also called persuasive essays, and *comparison* essays.

An argumentative essay is based on the writer's position on a certain topic and his/her evidence and evaluation of that evidence. It may also include a paragraph that presents a counterargument, showing that the writer is aware of other opinions of the subject.

A comparison essay is an analysis of two subjects or two aspects of a subject by pointing out similarities or/and differences. Comparison essays follow either a block pattern (subject-by-subject), or an alternating pattern (point-by-point). In the block pattern, the writer focuses on each subject separately, and then points out differences and/or similarities. In the alternating pattern, the writer focuses on both subjects together.

Ultimately, every essay has a title which is brief and illustrative of the essay's contents, such as "The Benefits of a Shared Language", "Language and Identity", "Literature as Mirror of Society", "Films as Sources of Learning."

116. ACTIVITY–STUDY AN ARGUMENTATIVE ESSAY

a. Study the following essay.

As history shows, it is not the number of speakers that makes a language global. Latin used to be a global language, not because it had the most number of speakers, but because of the power of the Roman Empire. The same is true about English, which became global due to the political, military, and economic power of the British Empire. But a language does not exist independently of its speakers, and the fact that English is such a dominating language shows that it is used in all domains of human interaction. In fact, a world language has numerous benefits in terms of political, economic, academic, and cultural communication across nations.

To begin with, having a global language ensures effective communication between different groups of people. Translations and oral interpretations have always been part of the international arena. Leaders, ambassadors, and businesspeople depended on translators and interpreters in their interactions with each other. But this limited their spontaneity in communication and led to various misunderstandings. In truth, communication mediated by translators bear a degree of cultural sensitivity, because translators are not always able to render accurately culturally specific expressions. A global language then offers a linguistically uniform platform where these challenges are discarded. Indeed, businesspeople in different parts of the world only have to reach for their phones or laptops to arrange a meeting. They do not need to travel long distances or spend time and money on what could be achieved from the comfort of their homes or offices.

Besides, a world language would be a welcome means in the world of international academia and the arts. Undeniably, academics are excited by the idea of reaching audiences outside national borders, providing lectures and seminars for learners from all over the globe. A conversation over the phone between a physicist in Norway with another in the U.S or Germany is achievable only with the help of a common language. If such an option was practical and regular, it would contribute greatly to the advancement of research and science. Furthermore, the arts would benefit enormously from a world language. It would make art be absorbed by huge audiences with no need for translations. Music, books, and films would preserve their original connotations, and they would appeal to the universality of human nature. In truth, people are more similar than we tend to believe, and a common language would facilitate the communication of these commonalities.

However, there are many voices that express concern over the danger of losing national languages. Many believe that language is closely connected to identity, and that language helps us to show where we belong and how we distinguish ourselves from other groups. It is the means by which we first experience the world, and it embodies our history, stories, songs, folktales, etc., and which determine who we are. However, the argument that a world language causes the loss of local languages is not necessarily justified. Good examples are French and Icelandic, which preserve their linguistic distinctiveness by using French or Icelandic equivalents to the widespread English words. Besides, it is worth remembering that English itself has borrowed numerous words from other languages throughout the centuries.

Ultimately, the benefits of a world language lie in creating mutual understanding among people and nations. But it does not exclude preserving cultural identity. Bilingualism is an achievable compromise - people get to keep their national languages and yet have a language which offers them access to the community of the world. Nobody would deny that by living in a monolingual world, one deprives oneself of access to a world of all kinds of possibilities.

b. Answer in complete sentences.

1. What is the topic of this essay?
2. What is the author's opinion about the topic?
3. What are the main aspects of the topic discussed in the essay?

c. Choose a suitable title for the essay.

1. English is Great
2. A Global Language for an Inclusive World
3. The Benefits of a Global Language

d. Share with the class.

e. Discuss in groups.

> What other benefits does a world language have?

117.   ACTIVITY–STUDY A COMPARISON ESSAY

a. Study the following essay.

A FULFILLING LIFE

What is a life worth living? This is the question that all human beings throughout history have asked themselves and tried to answer according to their own ideals. Many books and films deal with the question of what is important in life, what we should dedicate ourselves to, and what is worth pursuing. But is there a right answer for all human beings? When we look at literature, the answer is no. While some people believe that an ambitious life is the only one worth living, others prefer the comfort of a humble life. Examples to illustrate such different views are Nathaniel Hawthorne's short stories "The Ambitious Guest" and "The Great Stone Face".

Being remembered after death is the most important thing in life for the protagonist in "The Ambitious Guest". He is young and very ambitious, and he "could have borne to live an undistinguished life, but not to be forgotten in the grave." Indeed, nothing seems more important to him than going down in history as an exceptional man. He is thrilled at the thought that people will think of him as gifted and special, and will try to find out more about his life after he is gone. He longs for the glory that would "beam on all his pathway." The essence of life for him is to get recognition from the outside world. Other characters in the story can relate to his ambitions, they also had them at one time in their lives. But life turned out to be quite different from the way they imagined it. Yet, the end of the story reveals how ambitious pursuits can be futile.

Conversely, a quiet and unremarkable life is the choice of the protagonist in "The Great Stone Face". Ernest is an example of humbleness for everyone who knows him, with "a better wisdom than could be learned from books." It never occurs to him that his destiny is to become a prophetic figure, and that he will be admired by famous poets and philosophers of his time. He has a gentle wisdom about him, and he never asks for more than he already has. Even when famous people come to see the sage whose wisdom did not come from books, he continues to labor "for his bread, and was the same simple-hearted man that he had always been." Of course, the inhabitants of the valley where Ernest lives are not themselves aware of Ernest's remarkable character because of his simple life. This goes to show that people commonly view a successful life in the form of wealth and social prestige.

Obviously, the young man in "The Ambitious Guest" and Ernest in "The Great Stone Face" see different things worth pursuing in life. For the young man, an ambitious life is the ultimate form of a satisfying life, and achieving glory is the best way to live. For Ernest, however, life has value in doing good things for others, and enjoying the daily calmness of the present moment. While for the ambitious guest life is about self-realization and amassing personal achievements, for Ernest life is worth living in its meditative and unpretentious stream. What is more, the young guest considers a life of fame and glory the ultimate way to live, but he never gets to experience it. On the other hand, Ernest achieves fame without ever wishing for it. He has never been aware of how significant his life was for others, and that he will always be remembered as a remarkable symbol of wisdom.

Ultimately, the question of a meaningful life will never have a single answer. While for some a fulfilling life is to achieve success, for others, the comfort of a simple life is superior to everything else. One could easily argue that a meaningful life is one in which a person feels significant. However, it is up to everyone to decide whether that means to be significant for as many people as possible, or only for the people close to them. Getting acknowledgement is a stronger need in some than in others. But the truth is, as Samuel Butler puts it, "Life is like playing a violin solo in public and learning the instrument as one goes on."

b. Discuss in groups.

1. What is the topic of this essay?
2. What are the two subjects contrasted?
3. What are two main differences between the two subjects?

c. Share with the class.

d. Discuss in groups.

1. What does a meaningful life mean to you?
2. What is an ordinary life?
3. What is an extraordinary life?
4. Is it important to be remembered after death?

ESSAY DEVELOPMENT

Every essay has an introduction and a conclusion, which are the first and the last paragraphs of the essay respectively.

The introduction is a very important part of the essay. A good introduction grabs the reader's attention and interest in reading the essay. But the introduction also does the following three things:

   a. It introduces the topic of the essay.
   b. It presents the writer's opinion of that topic.
   c. It briefly names two or three points the essay will focus on.

A good introduction offers a clear idea of what follows in the essay. This is why many writers choose to write their introduction at the end, when they have an overview of their whole essay.

Each body paragraph deals with one aspect of the issue discussed in the essay. To keep a clear view of the structure and content of the paragraphs, it is best to have the first sentence of the paragraph as its main idea – the topic sentence. This means that the number of points discussed in the essay corresponds to the number of body paragraphs.

Dividing a text into paragraphs helps both the writer and the reader to keep a clear view of the argument and its logical flow. In other words, paragraphs delineate larger breaks in the essay in the same way sentences do in a paragraph. Besides, a new paragraph outlines a new point of view or a new step in the development of the argument. Each paragraph represents a distinct unit, focusing on one central thought. Therefore, the number of body paragraphs will correspond to the number of points the writer discusses in the essay.

The conclusion summarizes the main points discussed throughout the essay. It briefly reminds the reader what was promised in the introduction, and how this was achieved. Lastly, it may include a few final thoughts on the subject.

A well-written essay is clear and easily read. This is made possible by using linking words between sentences and paragraphs, which indicate how the next idea is related to the previous one, and how all sentences in the paragraph and all paragraphs in the essay are all part of one unit. Linking words such as *besides, moreover, in addition,* are meant to offer a similar idea to the one already mentioned. *However, on the other hand, yet* are words meant to show that an opposing idea follows.

118. ACTIVITY—IDENTIFY INTRODUCTION AND CONCLUSION

a. Study the following essay from which the introduction and conclusion are missing.

First, English as the only language would improve communication both locally and internationally among different cultures, religions, etc. Today's world is very different from the past, and people from various corners of the world find themselves living together. A lingua franca would not only remove the need to learn the local language. It would, in fact, help us to fully express who we are, which only a native tongue can presently do for us. We would be able to explain why, for example, we think or behave the way we do. Besides, a rich vocabulary would allow us to explain our opinions and the context we have formed them in. Consequently, many possible conflicts or prejudiced attitudes between people of different cultures would be avoided.

Moreover, a common language like English is the key to equal development and growth both on an individual and national level. It means that we could all have the same opportunities in terms of employment, education, technology, and science. Everybody in the world would benefit from the same opportunities to increase their standard of living. Career opportunities, for example, would not be limited to those available within national borders, and people would benefit from numerous prospects fitted to their competence and skills. In truth, it is common knowledge that the spread of a language is closely associated with political and cultural dominance. A shared language would reduce the economic and political inequality between countries, thus contributing to a more equal universal society.

Of course, some people may feel that the world is beautiful now because of its cultural and linguistic diversity, and that language is part of the beauty and identity of a country. But a shared language would offer the same culture and traditions for everybody to identify with. This would also strengthen solidarity between people and would make everyone feel part of a whole. There would no longer be a prevailing language which diminishes the authenticity of minority languages and cultures. There would be no more discrimination of other languages and nations, and everybody would feel part of a great welcoming culture.

b. Choose a suitable introduction for the essay above.

INTRODUCTION ONE

A world in which you benefit from job opportunities and education prospects across national borders is a very appealing world. A global language offers doctors worldwide the opportunity to exchange experiences and opinions about various medicines and treatments. A common language is essential in matters of international security, since countries need to cooperate daily in a globalized world.

INTRODUCTION TWO

Imagine a world in which you do not need to concern yourself with national barriers, and which offers unlimited access to different cultures worldwide. A world in which everybody uses one single language is a world in which communication and interaction between people and countries is effortless. A shared language would also facilitate growth and great understanding between nations.

c. Share in groups.

d. Choose a suitable conclusion for the essay above.

CONCLUSION ONE

All things considered, English is the ultimate means to achieve a better world in which there are no national barriers. A world with a single language is a world of more tolerance among people, as well as a world of equal growth and development. A common language could, in fact, be the desired factor to build a spirit of fellowship. It would ultimately make everybody feel a blissful belonging to the human race.

CONCLUSION TWO

By and large, there are many advantages to having a global language. You have the possibility to study and work at international institutions, such as universities or colleges. You can use English to learn about the latest developments and discoveries within science and technology. English offers access to international media, which updates us on what is going on around the world. English is also important in international politics, as it facilitates communication on significant issues between countries.

e. Share in groups.

f. Underline all linking words. Compare with a classmate.

g. Identify the task this essay is based on. Share with the class.

1. Write an argumentative essay in which you discuss the benefits of a global language.
2. Write an argumentative essay in which you comment on the following statement: *A world in which everybody speaks one shared language is a wonderful world.*
3. *One single language is all we need to make the world a peaceful place.* Write an essay in which you agree or disagree with this statement.

119. ACTIVITY–STUDY INTRODUCTIONS

a. Study the introductory paragraphs below.

INTRODUCTION ONE

The stages and directions of modern life are largely based on work values. We choose certain studies with the goals of a job-seeker in mind. We spend many hours a day at work, and are often preoccupied with work performance and excellence, which makes us anxious and stressed. This leaves us with limited time to spend with family and friends, and we rarely have the chance to explore life. Indeed, monotonous working days strip us of creativity and the opportunity to learn new things and seek new adventures. A post-work world would give us more time to spend with family and friends. It would allow us to focus on hobbies and pleasurable activities, and would offer us the freedom to use our days as we please.

INTRODUCTION TWO

Humans are activity-driven creatures. It is only by engaging in laborious activities and by producing tangible and practical things that we feel significant. For us, work is both potent and liberating. It offers meaningful ways to contribute to the good functioning of our community and the world. Work allows us to take control of our own lives, and create things of importance both for ourselves and others. It is through work that we meet people with the same skills as ourselves, which makes us feel that we belong and have value. A life without work would deprive us of the freedom to move up in the world, to structure our lives and gain self-worth.

b. Read the statements below and match them with the right introduction.

1. Life without work would feel terribly meaningless.
2. In a post-work world, life would be more meaningful.

c. Identify three aspects that each introduction proposes to discuss.

_____   _____
_____   _____
_____   _____

d. Share in groups.

120. ACTIVITY—WRITE AN INTRODUCTION

a. Study the following essay which lacks an introduction and a title.

(Introduction)

To begin with, people who belong to the upper class cannot relate to how the poor live and feel, because they know nothing about their lives. The rich try to avoid the poor and tend to show them no respect. They don't have the same moral values as the underprivileged in society. They enjoy their lives in luxury without feeling empathy or guilt for the poor. For example, the Sheridans in Katherine Mansfield's short story "The Garden Party" enjoy their party while a poor neighbor lies dead in a house not far away from their own. The Sheridans feel no guilt or sympathy for the widow and five children, who are grieving over their dead husband and father. Instead, they are concerned with the flowers, sandwiches, and clothes for the party. They are not willing to sacrifice their party for some poor people they do not know nor care about. Unfortunately, this is an example of how class differences create social and human distance between people in class societies.

Furthermore, the rich feel that they are entitled to their life of privileges. Adults encourage the barriers between the rich and the poor by teaching their children that these distinctions are important. Class differences affect our identity from when we are born, but they are strengthened by adults later in life. Parents have a huge role in forming their children's identity. For instance, the Burnells in Katherine Mansfield's short story "The Doll's House" live a life of luxury and don't want their children to have any contact with the poor Kelveys. We get to know about it when they let their children show the doll's house to all their friends, except the Kelvey girls. Even their teacher at school has a different kind of smile for the poor Kelveys, suggesting that they should be treated differently. It is obvious that Kezia, one of the Burnell girls, does not understand why this is so. Children have a kind and clear heart but, unfortunately, parents and the environment change their natural inclinations, teaching them to think that people with money are always better than others.

However, even if identity is closely connected to our social status, it doesn't mean that we have no control over our attitudes towards other people. Of course, our gender, appearance, and ethnicity are something we were born with. We learn from our family and environment how to conduct ourselves in society. But we are responsible ourselves for our attitudes and treatment of others. Being born in a certain family, social position, or country is not something we decided ourselves. It is something that has been given to us, and it is our duty to value and respect others who do not necessarily share our privileges and luck. We have to appreciate both what is good for ourselves and everyone around us.

Ultimately, even if our identity is largely influenced by our social class, adults have a great role in forming the identity and future of their children. By teaching children that their clothes, hobbies and activities make them better or worse than others, adults also teach them to adopt unfair attitudes and beliefs. It is, therefore, the responsibility of the parents to let children experience different people and circumstances regardless of their social standing. This is the only way to create a better understanding between people of different classes in the society.

b. **Discuss in groups.**

1. What is the topic of this essay?
2. What is the main idea in the first body paragraph?
3. What is the main idea in the second body paragraph?
4. What is the main idea in the third body paragraph?

c. **Write a suitable introduction. Begin with the topic of the essay, the writer's view of the topic and the three points discussed. Compare with a classmate.**

d. **Write a suitable title. Share with the class.**

121. ACTIVITY–WRITE A CONCLUSION

a. **Study the following essay (consisting of two body paragraphs) which lacks a conclusion.**

LITERATURE MIRRORS ITS SOCIETY

One of the greatest benefits of literature is its power to offer us valuable insights into different past times and societies. All literature is produced in certain historical contexts, and it largely reflects the social, economic and psychological issues of the time. And while history provides us with records of events, it does not appeal to us the way literature does. An illustrious example is the literature of the Victorian age, which depicts both the harsh life of the poor and the role of middle-class women in the Victorian society.

One of the most prominent writers to depict the problems of the Victorian age is Charles Dickens (1812-1870). In his famous novel "Oliver Twist," Dickens introduces us to London's low life through Oliver, a young boy who was born in a workhouse for the poor. Oliver's fate takes him into different lowlife segments of the English society. By reading "Oliver Twist", we learn about the workhouse system, which was established by The Poor Law of 1834 to deal with the increasing poor population in the British cities. When Oliver begs "Please, sir, I want some more," and as a result is threatened, "That boy will be hung", we witness the hunger and abuse poor children suffered. The novel also illustrates how the wealthy in society believed that the poor themselves were responsible for their lot. It is thus through the novel's informative perspective that we learn about the cruelty of the system at the time and the heartlessness of the more fortunate.

Another aspect of the mid-Victorian life and literature is the figure of the governess. In 1851, around 25,000 women were either teaching or taking care of other women's children. At the time, these were the only options of the educated middle-class women to earn their living. We learn about the life of such women in many Victorian novels, one of which is "Jane Eyre", written by Charlotte Brontë. The upper class employed a governess for centuries, but in the 19th century the wealthier segments of the middle class started to do the same. Paying a governess to teach the children of the family was a status symbol. By reading "Jane Eyre", we learn that a governess had to teach children "the usual branches of a good English education, together with French, Drawing, and Music", which were necessary accomplishments of an educated "lady" to find a suitable husband. Jane Eyre does not have a family of her own and is neither a servant nor a member of the family. She represents the prototype of the governess who does not quite fit in the family and is fairly unhappy most of the time.

[Conclusion]

b. Write a suitable conclusion for the essay by focusing on the two suggestions below.

1. Summarize in two sentences the writer's opinion about the topic.
2. Summarize in two sentences the main points of the topic.

c. Share in groups.

122. ACTIVITY—OFFER EXAMPLES AND DETAILS

a. Discuss in class.

> What would a world without work look like?

b. Study the introduction and half-finished body paragraphs below. Finish each body paragraph by offering details and examples which clarify the point of each paragraph.

The stages and directions of our modern life are largely based on work values. We choose certain studies with the goals of a job-seeker in mind. We spend many hours a day at work and are often preoccupied with work performance and excellence, which makes us anxious and stressed. This leaves us with limited time to spend with family and friends. We rarely have the chance to explore and enjoy life. Indeed, monotonous working days strip us of the creativity and opportunity to learn new things and explore new adventures. A post-work world would give us more time to spend with family and friends, focus on hobbies and pleasurable activities, as well as the freedom to organize our days as we please.

To begin with, we enter real life by being compelled to choose an education that would provide us with a job later. This is not necessarily something that comes naturally to many of us. People have different interests and skills which do not fit into a rigid pattern. Being compelled to pick a specific profession, many people find themselves squeezed into a web of limitations and wasted potential. In many countries education costs money, and students end up with a lot of debt upon their graduation. [Examples]

Moreover, work deprives us of a lot of time which we could spend with family and friends. Today's working days do not offer parents enough time to spend with their children. They simply do not have the energy necessary to take stock of what their children are concerned with, to participate in developing their interests, or even help them handle the challenges of daily life. Similarly, adults do not have time to spend with their elderly parents, ask for advice and just reminisce over life's meaning and its joys. [Examples]

Above all, however, a world of no work would offer us time for self-actualization. We would be able to learn about the things that we are genuinely interested in, explore what we are good at, and engage in activities that bring us joy. We would have the chance to discover hidden talents and skills, and be able to create more while consuming less. Today's work-focused world does not allow us to be creative enough, but in a world where work is not the heart of life, we could let imagination run wild and explore the things and people on a much larger scale. [Examples]

c. **Write a suitable conclusion for the essay by focusing on the two suggestions below.**

1. Summarize in two sentences the writer's opinion about work discussed in the essay.
2. Summarize in two or three sentences the main points of the topic.

d. **Write a suitable title.**

e. **Compare your examples, conclusion and title with a classmate's.**

123. ACTIVITY–OFFER EXAMPLES AND DETAILS

a. **Discuss in class.**

What are the greatest benefits of work in our lives?

a. **Study the introduction and half-finished body paragraphs below. Finish each body paragraph by offering details and examples which clarify the point of each paragraph.**

Humans are activity-driven creatures. It is only by engaging in laborious activities and by producing tangible and practical things that we feel significant. Work is both potent and liberating, as it offers meaningful ways to contribute to the good functioning of our community and the world. Work makes us take control of our own lives, and create things of importance both for ourselves and others. It is through work that we meet people with the same skills as ourselves, which makes us feel that we belong and have value. A life without work would deprive us of the freedom to move up in the world, to structure our life and gain self-esteem.

First, work offers solutions to unfairness and inequality so prevalent in societies. Being born in a less privileged social position does not need to be final, as work offers us the chance to better our lot. We can always learn a vocation and work hard to achieve great results in our field of work. In this way, we are appreciated and respected for our skills and expertise, and not for where we come from. Work allows us to become self-reliant and resourceful. *[Examples]*

Next, work offers us structure, as it provides us with routines and clear time frames, which helps us to be organized and goal-oriented. We know what our tasks are and how we should go about our time to perform them efficiently. Work serves not only as a time management, but also guides us to self-improvement. It is no secret that many people struggle with managing their time and energy in an ordered manner, as it is easy to get distracted in a world of distractions. *[Examples]*

Most importantly, however, work is the pathway to self-worth. Even if we do not possess a special skill or talent, we can always work hard to achieve vocational excellence. Thus, we are appreciated for our knowledge and abilities, as well as our efforts. We receive acknowledgement in the form of financial remuneration, as well as social and professional prestige. This in return motivates us to hone our skills, broaden our knowledge and expertise, and consequently, feel valuable and meaningful. What is more, work offers us the opportunity to meet people with the same skills as ourselves.

> Examples

b. Write a suitable conclusion for the essay by focusing on the two suggestions below.

1. Summarize in two sentences the writer's opinion about work discussed in the essay.
2. Summarize in two or three sentences the main points of the topic.

c. Write a suitable title.

d. Compare your examples, conclusion and title with a classmate's.

124. ACTIVITY–STUDY ESSAY STRUCTURE

a. Discuss in class.

- What is the difference between attitude and behavior?
- Do attitudes always predict behavior?

b. Study the following text.

Our attitudes involve evaluations of the world. These evaluations are based on beliefs and manifested in feelings. But most importantly, attitudes include inclinations to act. They are guiding our understanding and reactions to the world. Yale University researchers suggest that there are three dimensions of attitudes: emotional, behavioral, and cognitive. In other words, attitudes include *feeling*, *doing* and *thinking*. Attitudes and behavior have generally been considered closely connected. The belief was that by examining a person's attitude, we can predict that person's behavior. Recent psychological research, however, reveals that the relationship between attitudes and behavior is more complex, and in fact, there are situations when behavior determines attitudes.

According to behaviorist theory, we form attitudes through direct experience with an object. When our experience of an object is positive, we form positive attitudes toward it. For example, psychologists Addison and Thorpe found that people who had direct positive experiences with mentally ill persons have developed positive attitudes towards mental illness in general. Social learning theory suggests that we form attitudes by directly observing other people. In this case, other people serve as models and the consequences of their behavior are the basis of our attitudes. For instance, children imitate their parents' and other adults' behavior and learn patterns of behavior based on rewarding or punishing consequences. In addition, we engage in a process of social comparison in which we test the legitimacy of our views and base them on those of other people. This happens when we are undecided about what our attitudes should be.

Social psychologists agree that attitudes help us size up our social world and provide us with information about how to respond to it. Attitudes help us pay attention to what is important in our environment. They help us remember, make decisions, and categorize people and things in meaningful ways. For example, my conscientious attitude to school subjects make me pay attention to what the teacher says in class. My attitude toward meat-eating helps me choose easily vegetarian dishes in a restaurant. By categorizing a person as elderly on the bus, I offer them my seat. In addition, attitudes serve as defense mechanisms against anxiety, and reinforce our sense of self. For instance, by portraying myself as self-assured, I can make others trust me. I can also present a certain self-image to the world by demonstrating attitudes I consider important.

It might be intuitive to think that attitudes predict behavior but this is not always the case. Social psychologists have found that there is little correspondence between words and actions when the attitude is general and the behavior specific. For example, the American sociologist Richard LaPierre showed in a famous study that attitudes do not predict behavior. He traveled with a Chinese couple in a time with strong anti-Chinese feelings throughout the US. During their travels, they were denied housing only once. But when LaPierre later wrote to the same guest houses and camps and asked whether they would accept Chinese guests, more than 90% said "No". General attitudes include subjective norms about what other people think about the behavior. Therefore, they can be based on social norms and observations of others.

We often come to believe in what we say rather than say what we believe in. Studies show that in the absence of disconfirming evidence, we come to believe in what we say. According to cognitive dissonance theory, we constantly tend to justify our actions to ourselves. Whenever our behavior is inconsistent with our attitude, we adjust our attitude to fit our action. For example, if you were rude to a classmate, you would feel bad about it later. However, to escape the unpleasant thoughts about it, you will justify your behavior by telling yourself that your classmate surely wronged you, and your reaction was legitimate. Furthermore, self-perception theory suggests that we assume that our actions are self-revelatory. So, when we are uncertain about our beliefs or feelings, we look at our actions for answers. This motivates us to believe in what we have done, and that our actions represent our attitudes.

c. Match each heading with the right paragraph.

- The functions of attitudes
- We look at actions to explain beliefs
- When attitudes are inconsistent with behavior
- How we form attitudes
- Defining attitudes

CITE EVIDENCE

School assignments are generally based on questions that ask to analyze, discuss, argue, and clarify a subject. This implies a great deal of research and evaluation of sources. A well-written essay is based on information from reliable sources.

One of the most critical things when you write, however, is to be cautious about plagiarism. Plagiarism refers to using words, phrases, or entire sentences without referring to their authorship. Plagiarism is intellectual theft and has harsh consequences. Therefore, it is crucial that you always reference the sources that you use in your own writing. Use quotation marks when you cite direct phrases and sentences or rephrase ideas by mentioning their source.

Most assignments ask explicitly that you give evidence from relevant texts (both factual and literary texts) and films to support your thoughts and viewpoints. Therefore, every claim you make must be based on evidence found in appropriate texts and films to communicate to the reader the validity of your arguments. To do this, you have to select details and examples that support your ideas. These you can either cite directly from the text or paraphrase.

EXAMPLE OF DIRECT CITATION
Charles Dickens is considered a giant of the world literature because of his insight into the human psyche and how it is molded by history. "Whatever the word "great" means, Dickens was that word", declares English writer and philosopher G. K. Chesterton when examining the men with the greatest influence in literature. Chesterton proclaims Dickens an intellectual titan, capable of anticipating the changes coming in the British society "much more soberly and scientifically than did his better educated and more pretentious contemporaries."

EXAMPLE OF PARAPHRASE
Original text: "Life is like playing a violin solo in public and learning the instrument as one goes on. One cannot make the best of such impossibilities, and the question is doubly fatuous until we are told which of our two lives— the conscious or the unconscious— is held by the asker to be the truer life. Which does the question contemplate— the life we know, or the life which others may know, but which we know not?"
Paraphrase: Samuel Butler believes that life is like a public performance with everybody watching us while we live it. There is no pre-planned life course, and we make decisions along the way, which ultimately form our existence. Besides, the life we know as ours is different from the life others see, which makes our own perception of our life different from everybody else's.

125. ACTIVITY–STUDY AN EXAMPLE ESSAY

a. Read the following introduction.

Imagine a world in which work is only a tiny insignificant part of your day. Work is there for you to exercise your skills, to contribute to the good functioning of society, but it is not your whole life. Life consists mostly of leisure and you are the master of your own time. There are no urgent tasks you have to complete at work and no anxiety about the need to be an efficient and productive employee. Would a world with very little work be an ideal world? Many thinkers throughout history have extolled the need for idleness, and have criticized busyness for ruining what human life is about – enjoying the present moment.

b. What is the topic of this essay? What aspects of the topic do you expect to read further on? Write key words or sentences.

c. Read the first body paragraph.

In his essay "In Praise of Idleness," Bertrand Russell declares that "there is far too much work in the world, that immense harm is caused by the belief that work is virtuous." In fact, happiness and prosperity lie in the reduction of work. The philosopher claims that work is the means by which the exploiters and the rich maintain their life of privileges. The wealthy have always used work as an excuse for keeping the poor away from immoral habits, believing that the poor have no imagination about how to use their time. But by reducing the role of work in society, everybody, not only the rich, would have time to appreciate life more. Life would consist of more than hard work in order to "secure the necessaries of life." It would not only make everybody happier, it would also create a fairer society, in which everybody has the right to enjoy themselves. To be sure, idleness is just as harmful as overwork, but Russell proposes that four hours of work a day would offer everybody the chance to be playful, to engage in hobbies, and to experience small pleasures in life.

d. What is the main idea of the paragraph?

e. Read the second body paragraph.

In her novel "Adam Bede," George Elliot decries the fast pace of life caused by the Industrial Revolution and expresses concern over the death of leisure. "Ingenious philosophers tell you, perhaps, that the great work of the steam-engine is to create leisure for mankind. Do not believe them: it only creates a vacuum for eager thought to rush in." The author believes that leisure is essential for well-founded thinking and that being in a rush creates an absence of thought. When deprived of the time to reflect over things, one tends to act impulsively, while leisure makes people reflective and happy in their "inability to know the causes of things, preferring the things themselves." The increase of work and busyness is seen by Elliot as stressful because it makes people restless and for ever in pursuit of an unknown goal. Work truly creates competitiveness and an ambitious way of life, causing both anxiety and insecurity. Or as the author puts it, when leisurely times are gone, people become "squeamish[3] by doubts and lofty aspirations." Life is thus seen as a demanding task rather than stress-free enjoyment.

f. **What is the main idea of the paragraph?**

g. **Read the third body paragraph.**

In his essay "Life at High Pressure," English essayist William Greg cautions us that a life of abundant work and pressure is bad for our health and strength. Excess does not sit well with human nature, and we are bound to pay the price eventually. But most importantly, while devoting life to business and professional life, people also "lose all capability of a better life, all relish[4] for recreation or contemplation," which is essential to a good life. Too much work weakens our abilities to enjoy free time and relaxation, and it becomes hard to disconnect from the world of duties, tasks, and productivity. It is wrong to teach children and youths that work is the only thing that matters and that accumulation of achievements and wealth is the only way to succeed. For a meaningful life is a life in which we stop and think whether the things we need are the same as the ones we chase. Less work means more time to reflect on "what is the value, and the purpose, and *the price* of what we have seen, and done, and visited." When we fail to do so, we can hardly live "an adequate or worthy life."

h. **What is the main idea of the paragraph?**

Finally, even if work has always been part of social life, it should not be made the final destination, nor should it be the way we live our lives. It is true that human happiness consists of needs, some of which are met through work, but most needs are a contemplation of what matters. Human flourishing is not based on being productive but rather valuable. While work makes us part of a whole, leisure offers us time to be by ourselves. To make life worthwhile, we should stop and smell the roses.

i. **Choose the most suitable title.**

1. Happiness Is Found in Leisure Hours
2. A Better Life with Less Work
3. Idleness Is the Answer to The Good Life

---

[3] Squeamish – nervous, put off
[4] Relish – great enjoyment, satisfaction, appreciation

j. **Share your answers in groups.**

126. ACTIVITY–VOCABULARY PRACTICE

a. **Match the words on the left with their synonyms on the right. Compare with a classmate.**

1. Shrouds		a.	Serious
2. Ends		b.	To rise
3. Solemn		c.	Goals
4. Seem		d.	Be burdened with
5. Be cursed		e.	Do injustice to
6. Blank		f.	Clothes
7. To wrong		g.	To form
8. Means		h.	Very small
9. To stead		i.	Look
10. To climb		j.	Clean
11. To shape		k.	Methods
12. Tiny		l.	To help

b. **Discuss in groups.**

1. What are the consequences of encouraging women to focus on their looks rather than on their intellect?
2. Is there power in a woman's physical charms?
3. Comment the quote: "The less a woman has in her head, the lighter she is for climbing."

(Answer key, inverted at bottom of page:)

Shrouds	Clothes
Ends	Goals
Solemn	Serious
Seem	Look
Be cursed	Be burdened with
Blank	Clean
To wrong	Do injustice to
Means	Methods
To stead	To help
To climb	To rise
To shape	To form
Tiny	Very small

127. ACTIVITY–CITE EVIDENCE

The excerpt below is taken from the novel "The Story of an African Farm" (1883) by South African author Olive Schreiner. In it, Lyndall, a reflective girl who holds unconventional views about gender roles, talks to Waldo, a serious and studious person. She talks about the way women are viewed as inferior to men, who are never valued for their brains and only for their physical appearance.

a. Study the following excerpt.

"But we are cursed. Waldo, born cursed from the time our mothers bring us into the world till the shrouds are put on us. Do not look at me as though I were talking nonsense. Everything has two sides— the outside that is ridiculous, and the inside that is solemn." "I am not laughing," said the boy, sedately enough; "but what curses you?" He thought she would not reply to him, she waited so long. "It is not what is done to us, but what is made of us," she said at last, "that wrongs us. No man can be really injured but by what modifies himself. We all enter the world little plastic beings, with so much natural force, perhaps, but for the rest— blank. And the world tells us what we are to be, and shapes us by the ends it sets before us. To you it says: "Work," and to us it says: "Seem!" To you it says: As you approximate to man's highest ideal of God, as your arm is strong and your knowledge great, and the power to labour is with you, so you shall gain all that human heart desires. To us it says: Strength shall not help you, nor knowledge, nor labour. You shall gain what men gain, but by other means. And so, the world makes men and women. "Look at this little chin of mine, Waldo, with the dimple in it. It is but a small part of my person, but though I had a knowledge of all things under the sun, and the wisdom to use it, and the deep loving heart of an angel, it would not stead me through life like this little chin. I can win money with it, I can win love; I can win power with it, I can win fame. What would knowledge help me? The less a woman has in her head the lighter she is for climbing. I once heard an old man say, that he never saw intellect help a woman so much as a pretty ankle; and it was the truth. They begin to shape us to our cursed end," she said, with her lips drawn in to look as though they smiled, "when we are tiny things in shoes and socks. We sit with our little feet drawn up under us in the window, and look out at the boys in their happy play. We want to go. Then a loving hand is laid on us: 'Little one, you cannot go,' they say, 'your little face will burn, and your nice white dress be spoiled.'

Olive Schreiner, *The Story of an African Farm*

b. Discuss in groups: What are the main ideas of the text?

c. Write a paragraph that begins with the topic sentence suggested. Cite evidence from the text above.

Throughout history, men kept women in a subordinate position by encouraging them to focus on their looks rather than their brains.

128. ACTIVITY–VOCABULARY PRACTICE

a. Match the words to the left with their synonyms to the right. Compare with a classmate.

1. Enslave		a.	Harm
2. Cramp		b.	Determined passion
3. Sharpen		c.	Assumptions
4. Mischief		d.	Social behavior
5. Disregard		e.	Intelligence
6. Disorderly		f.	Ambition
7. Guesswork		g.	Hinder
8. By snatches		h.	Enhance
9. Persevering ardour		i.	Oppress
10. Corporeal		j.	Indifference
11. Emulation		k.	Principles of behavior
12. Sagacity		l.	Unsystematic
13. Fortified		m.	Fragmentary
14. Manners		n.	Bodily
15. Morals		o.	Stimulated

b. Discuss in groups.

1. Describe a systematic education versus an unsystematic one.
2. How does an understanding of the world based on personal reflection differ from an understanding based on manners learned from others?
3. Comment on: *When you are deprived of reflecting on the meaning of things, you become prey for prejudices, and make others' opinions your own.*

Enslave	Oppress
Cramp	Hinder
Sharpen	Enhance
Mischief	Harm
Disregard	Indifference
Disorderly	Unsystematic
Guesswork	Assumptions
By snatches	Fragmentary
Persevering ardour	Determined passion
Corporeal	Bodily
Emulation	Ambition
Sagacity	Intelligence
Fortified	Stimulated
Manners	Social behavior
Morals	Principles of behavior

129. ACTIVITY–CITE EVIDENCE

The excerpt below is taken from "A Vindication of the Rights of Woman" (1792) by Mary Wollstonecraft. It was the first great feminist piece of literature, which still strikes a chord today and resonates with the human rights movement.

a. Study the following excerpt.

Many are the causes that contribute to enslave women by cramping their understandings and sharpening their senses. One, perhaps, that silently does more mischief than all the rest, is their disregard of order… women, who, generally speaking, receive only a disorderly kind of education, seldom attend to with that degree of exactness that men, who from their infancy are broken into method, observe. This negligent kind of guesswork prevents their generalizing matters of fact, so they do today what they did yesterday, merely because they did it yesterday. Led by their dependent situation and domestic employments more into society, what they learn is rather by snatches; and as learning is with them, in general, only a secondary thing, they do not pursue any one branch with that persevering ardour necessary to give vigour to the faculties, and clearness to the judgment. But in the education of women the cultivation of the understanding is always subordinate to the acquirement of some corporeal accomplishment. Besides, in youth their faculties are not brought forward by emulation; and having no serious scientific study, if they have natural sagacity it is turned too soon on life and manners. As a proof that education gives this appearance of weakness to females, we may instance the example of military men, who are, like them, sent into the world before their minds have been stored with knowledge or fortified by principles. The great misfortune is this, that they both acquire manners before morals, and a knowledge of life before they have from reflection. The consequence is natural; satisfied with common nature, they become prey to prejudices, and taking all their opinions on credit, they blindly submit to authority.
    Mary Wollstonecraft. *A Vindication of the Rights of Woman* (504-520; 534-538).

b. Discuss in groups. What are the main ideas of the text?

c. Write a paragraph that begins with the topic sentence suggested. Cite evidence from the text above.

> *As long as women do not get the same kind of education as men, they have no chance of changing the social roles they have.*

130. ACTIVITY–VOCABULARY PRACTICE

a. Match the words on the left with their synonyms on the right. Compare with a classmate.

1. Admire
2. Dreadful
3. Misery
4. Wickedness
5. Invent
6. Cruelty
7. Wither
8. Uproar
9. Moan
10. Quench

a. Disturbance
b. Reduce
c. Create
d. Applaud
e. Terrible
f. Weaken
g. Unhappiness
h. Sob
i. Evil
j. Viciousness

b. Discuss in groups.

1. Why are women associated with tenderness and men with aggressiveness?
2. Would there be more love in a world ruled by women?
3. How would the world be like if female leaders were equal to male leaders?

> Admire — Applaud
> Dreadful — Terrible
> Misery — Unhappiness
> Wickedness — Evil
> Invent — Create
> Cruelty — Viciousness
> Wither — Weaken
> Uproar — Disturbance
> Moan — Sob
> Quench — Reduce

131. ACTIVITY–CITE EVIDENCE

The excerpt below is taken from the novel "The Bostonians" (1886) by American author Henry James. In it, Verena Tarrant, a very good public speaker, is delivering a speech "about the gentleness and goodness of women, and how, during the long ages of history, they had been trampled under the iron heel of man. It was about their day having come at last, about the universal sisterhood, about their duty to themselves and to each other."

a. Study the following excerpt.

"Of course, I only speak to women— to my own dear sisters; I don't speak to men, for I don't expect them to like what I say. They pretend to admire us very much, but I should like them to admire us a little less and to trust us a little more. I don't know what we have ever done to them that they should keep us out of everything. When I see the dreadful misery of mankind and think of the suffering of which at any hour, at any moment, the world is full, I say they had better let us come in a little and see what we can do. Poverty, and ignorance, and crime; disease, and wickedness, and wars! To kill each other, with all sorts of expensive and perfected instruments, that is the most brilliant thing they have been able to invent. It seems to me that we might stop it, we might invent something better. The cruelty— the cruelty; there is so much, so much! Why shouldn't tenderness come in? Why should our woman's hearts be so full of it, and all so wasted and withered, while armies and prisons and helpless miseries grow greater all the while? It is what the great sisterhood of women might do if they should all join hands, and lift up their voices above the brutal uproar of the world, in which it is so hard for the plea of mercy or of justice, the moan of weakness and suffering, to be heard. We should quench it, we should make it still, and the sound of our lips would become the voice of universal peace! For this we must trust one another, we must be true and gentle and kind. We must remember that the world is ours too, ours— little as we have ever had to say about anything!— and that the question is not yet definitely settled whether it shall be a place of injustice or a place of love!"

Henry James. The Bostonians, Vol. I (of II) (880-898).

b. Discuss in groups: What are the main ideas of the text?

c. Write a paragraph that begins with the topic sentence suggested. Cite evidence from the text above.

The world would be a much better place if women were equal to men in all spheres of life.

---

132. ACTIVITY–WRITE AN ESSAY BY GIVING EVIDENCE

a. Read the introduction below which will be part of an essay you are going to write. It has the following title: *Women as Partners and not Subordinates*.

Throughout most of human history, inequality has been a part of social life. There have always been people who have more power, and thus more privileges, in society. This also implies that people in power decide the lives of those less privileged, and therefore create cultural norms which perpetuate unequal social relationships. One type of inequality is gender inequality, in which men hold better positions than women in society. Consequently, men keep women outside the decision-making processes, and in this way, prevent them from exercising their intellectual capabilities. This has been historically done by encouraging women to focus on their looks rather than their intelligence, and by depriving women of a systematic and orderly education. A world in which women decide affairs equally with men would be a much better world.

   b. **Write three body paragraphs in which you discuss the topic sentences provided. Cite evidence and use linking words.**

To begin with, men kept women in a subordinate position by encouraging them to focus on their looks instead of their intellect.

   Actually, as long as women do not get the same kind of education as men, they have no chance of changing the social roles they have.

The truth is that the world would be a much better place if women were equal to men in all spheres of social life.

   c. **Write a conclusion. You may use the introduction to help you summarize the main points. The conclusion should briefly indicate how everything promised in the introduction has been satisfactorily discussed.**

HOW TO READ A TASK

Understanding the question of a task is the first and most important step in writing your essay. You should spend some time on reading it carefully and never rush to answer it only because you feel you know a lot about the topic.

Three things are vital to consider when you read an assignment:

- Examine carefully the key words in the text of the task. For example, in a task which presents a statement such as, "Prejudices are based on fears of the unknown," the key words are *prejudices* and *fears*. This means that your essay should reveal and discuss the connection between the two concepts, and how people's prejudices and their fears of the unknown are related.

- Look closely for instruction words in the text of the task. For example, when you are asked to *discuss* a topic or issue, you are asked to use your reasoning skills and select relevant evidence to make a case for or against an argument or specify the advantages and disadvantages of a given situation/issue. Besides, all task texts include key words which indicate the aspects you must focus in your essay. It is of paramount importance that you identify them before you start planning your writing.

- You should think of specific sources (factual texts, short stories, poems, films) which you can use as evidence to support your ideas. For example, when the task includes words such as *prejudices* and *fears*, you should think of texts or films which deal with these themes and how they relate to the viewpoint you are going to put forward.

It is sometimes easy to stray from the question of the assignment, as there may be so much more you know and want to say about the topic. Yet, it is crucial that you frequently stop and reread the assignment: are you doing what it asks you to do? Are you focusing on the specific aspects indicated in the text of the task? It is worth making connections between the present and earlier tasks, as it may help you stay focused on what is relevant.

133. ACTIVITY–STUDY TASKS

a. **Study the following tasks. Underline key words in the text. Explain in two or three sentences what each task asks you to discuss/reflect on.**

TASK 1. When easily forgiven, people fail to learn responsibility.
_____ _____
_____ _____

TASK 2. Sometimes, forgiving is encouraging the person to make the same mistake again.
_____ _____
_____ _____

TASK 3. Sometimes, revenge is more beneficial than forgiveness.
_____ _____
_____ _____

b. **Choose suitable aspects/questions that match each task.**

1. What are the consequences of forgiving easily?
2. What is the relation between anger and self-respect?
3. How do people react when they are forgiven?
4. When do people make the same mistake again?
5. Who benefits more from forgiving: the wrongdoer or the victim?
6. When do people fail to learn from their mistakes?
7. When does revenge teach a lesson?
8. What are the benefits of anger?
9. What are the circumstances that make us become responsible?
10. How does being easily forgiven deprive us of taking responsibility?
11. What makes forgiving easy (causes)?
12. When is revenge a better lesson than forgiveness?

134. ACTIVITY–STRUCTURE AN ESSAY

a. **Study the following introduction. Underline three points that will be discussed in the essay. Compare with a classmate.**

Forgiveness is one of the most important elements of human life. People make mistakes all the time, but for the sake of human relations, we need to be able to let go of negative feelings and abandon painful memories. In its deepest meaning, to forgive is to accept what it means to be human, and it makes coexistence with other people a pleasant experience. Even if forgiveness may be difficult to achieve, it offers valuable life lessons in tolerance, it brings peace of mind and removes hostility.

b. Study the following three topic sentences. Match them with the right body paragraph below.

1. One of the great advantages of forgiveness is to eliminate hatred and hostility.
2. When you forgive, you offer a person a lesson in tolerance.
3. Forgiveness offers gratification by forging an agreeable relationship between you and the wrongdoer.

A.
It may even make the wrongdoer repent and avoid making the same mistake again. Besides, forgiving somebody teaches that person to forgive in return. One such example is the short story "Thank you Ma'am" by Langston Hughes. When Roger tries to steal Mrs. Luella's purse, she doesn't become angry or hand him over to the police. Instead, she takes him home and gives him food. Rather than blaming and criticizing him, Mrs. Luella treats him kindly, and thus makes a wise decision. In this way, she teaches him to behave like a good and kind person in the future. Her decision will leave a good impression on him and will teach him the difference between right and wrong. He also learns that he is responsible for his actions.

B.
There is no doubt that when you forgive, you rid yourself of feelings of anger and grief. Sometimes, thinking about another person other than yourself can make you understand that people see the world differently, and this is why they behave in different ways. On the contrary, by not forgiving, we do not even try to understand, and thus wrongly believe that there is only one way a person should act. This then becomes a source of frustration and unhappiness. Besides, when you forgive, you generate positive feelings not only for yourself but also for those around you. One example is the short story "Going Home" by Pete Hamill. After spending four years in prison and not knowing whether he still has a family, Vingo finds out that his wife has forgiven him. We may speculate that she has done it because she loves him or maybe because she has the interest of their children in mind. Regardless, when she forgives Vingo, she ensures the safety of herself and her children, thus strengthening the nature of their relationship.

C.
Refusing to forgive can result in a life of depression, anxiety and insecurity. Sometimes, it is hard to forgive, but you have to do it in order to live in peace. One example to illustrate this are the horrible atrocities committed by the Australian government against the Aborigines. They tried to eradicate a whole race by forcibly taking the Aboriginal children away from their parents. Undoubtedly, the most difficult thing is to take a child from their mother's bosom, and the story of the Stolen Generations is indeed a black mark in the Australian history. However, current generations should forgive this part of history not because they have not experienced the cruel actions themselves, but because it would mean avoiding destructive conflicts and animosity.

In conclusion, forgiveness offers far more benefits than the ones mentioned above. Most importantly, though, forgiveness builds harmonious relationships between people and nations, and it prevents hostility and bitterness. It is important to remember that life is short and it is not worth spending it thinking about what others have done to you. To live peacefully with other human beings, you must be kind to them, and forgive those who have hurt you.

c. Use the linking words below to connect the three body paragraphs.

Finally, to begin with, in addition

d. Share in groups.

e. Which of the following tasks is this essay based on?

1. When you forgive, you decide that the past is less important than the future. Write an argumentative essay in which you discuss this statement.
2. *To believe in rightness clashes with the ability to forgive.* Write an argumentative essay in which you discuss this statement.
3. When people are easily forgiven, they are deprived of the opportunity to become responsible individuals. Write an argumentative essay in which you discuss this statement.
4. It is undeniable that forgiveness is beneficial for our well-being. Write an argumentative essay in which you discuss this statement.

f. Choose a suitable title.

1. To Forgive is to Understand
2. The Upsides of Forgiveness
3. Forgiveness Offers Lessons in Humility

g. Share with the class.

135. ACTIVITY–STUDY TASKS

a. Work in groups.

Read the tasks below and underline key words important to consider when writing an argumentative essay. Prepare an outline by thinking about three points you can discuss in each task. Follow the example below.

TASK 1.

A society in which people do not look after each other is a society of conflicts and mistrust. Write an argumentative essay in which you discuss this statement by referring to relevant texts/films.

Introduction	<ul><li>introduce the topic</li><li>introduce opinion of the topic</li><li>introduce the main points that will be discussed</li></ul>
1	<ul><li>discuss how lack of responsibility is connected to conflicts</li><li>give examples of situations in which conflicts arise because people pursue their own interests</li></ul>
2	<ul><li>discuss how responsibility is connected to mistrust</li><li>give examples of situations in which a lack of responsibility leads to human interactions based on suspicion and doubt</li></ul>
3	<ul><li>discuss some solutions</li><li>how can conflicts and mistrust be reduced in society by taking more responsibility for each other?</li></ul>
Conclusion	<ul><li>sum up main points, write a few final thoughts</li></ul>

Things to remember!

Relevant text/film: *An Inspector Calls*

- ✓ Find good examples from relevant texts to support my claims
- ✓ Use linking words to show the logical flow of my ideas
- ✓ Use synonyms for words/concepts important in the essay

TASK 2.

Prejudice is both a matter of ignorance and laziness, as we judge people without knowing them and we do not bother to use reason to control our instinctual reactions.

Write an argumentative essay in which you discuss this statement by referring to relevant texts/films.

> RELEVANT FILM
> *Crash*

TASK 3.

It takes courage and personal sacrifice to fight for a more equal society.

Write an argumentative essay in which you discuss this statement by referring to relevant texts/films.

> RELEVANT FILMS
> *Selma*
> *Iron Jawed Angels*

   b. **Share with the class.**

136. ACTIVITY- IDENTIFY TASK AND DETAILS

   a. **Read the introduction and conclusion below.**

INTRODUCTION

We are all members of a social organism in which everyone is dependent on each other. Of course, people of means tend to be reluctant to share their privileges with the less fortunate. They generally believe that the poor deserve their lot and should be left to fend for themselves. But they too are part of the same social organism and are not immune to misfortunes. It may seem like a scary thought, but being held responsible for all your actions may actually make you more mindful, help guide your moral behavior, and offer a support network should you ever need it.

CONCLUSION

Ultimately, people are only responsible for their own actions, and the only thing that they can control is their reaction. But this only goes to show that if everybody is conscious of their constant responsibility to others, then regard for their wellbeing becomes the rule everybody lives by. A society in which all individuals are concerned with the well-being of others is a healthy society. Social life is like a social body in which every organ makes sure the others operate well because it is the only way it can properly function.

b. Study the following tasks and choose the task that the introduction and conclusion above are based on. Work in groups.

Task 1. *We cannot let others' misfortunes influence our own happiness.* Write an argumentative essay in which you discuss this statement.

Task 2. *Being responsible for everyone we ever met and everything we ever did is a horrible thought.* Write an argumentative essay in which you discuss this statement.

Task 3. *I am, of course, responsible for my own happiness above everyone and everything else.* Write an argumentative essay in which you discuss this statement.

c. What is the author's opinion about the statement in the task? Write it here. Share with the class.

d. What are the three points the author is going to focus on? (*hint: you find them in the last sentence of the paragraph*) **Underline them. Share with the class.**

e. Study the topic sentences corresponding to the three body paragraphs below.

1. Being responsible for all your actions makes you mindful of what you say and do in your daily life.
2. By the same token, being held responsible for your actions makes you behave morally towards others, irrespective of their social standing.
3. But whether privileged or underprivileged, no human being is safe from misfortunes.

f. Match each topic sentence with its appropriate supporting sentences.

A.
Life is highly unpredictable and what one has today is no guaranteed to be there tomorrow. We are never prepared for the inevitably tragic moments of life. But when we look after one another, the anxiety of potential calamities is highly reduced, because we know we can rely on our fellow men and women. All individuals have certain social roles,

which also implies that we are limited in how much we can do. But this is why it is so important for people to rely on the role of somebody else to help them when in need. Impoverished people like Eva Smith need the rich to offer them assistance and understanding when they struggle to make ends meet.

B.

It also makes you compassionate and understanding towards other people. Knowing you are responsible for the way you treat others makes you thoughtful of the things they struggle with, which you know nothing about. It seemed ridiculous to him to care about her troubles. He was only looking out for his own interests as an employer and businessman. Similarly, his wife, Mrs. Birling, felt no responsibility to find out more about Eva's situation. She mistrusted her because of her preconceptions of the poor and unmarried girls who become pregnant. Their disregard for the girl's situation, and the belief that they have no responsibility for anyone but themselves, had tragic consequences on the poor girl's life.

C.

It is tempting to act dishonestly when nobody can hold you accountable for your actions. It is easy to take advantage of people who are vulnerable and who do not have the social and economic capital to protect themselves. But Sheila also exhibits the same kind of superiority when she is in the shop, as she seems oblivious to the consequences her complaining would have on Eva Smith's life situation. Mrs. Birling herself can easily be accused of being hypocritical in her attitude towards Eva Smith. She harshly condemns the man responsible for leaving her with child, but changes her mind when she discovers that the man is her son. Had they all been aware of the seriousness of their actions, and that they could be held accountable for them, their behaviors – hopefully – would have had a different nature.

g. **Share with the class.**

h. **The three exemplifying/supporting sentences below are each part of one of the body paragraphs above. Set them in the right place within the paragraph.**

   1. For example, both Gerald and Eric in "An Inspector Calls" take advantage of their social standing to exploit their unequal relationship with Eva Smith.
   2. Wealthy people like the Birlings in J. B. Priestley's play, for example, need poor people to perform jobs in their factories.
   3. Mr. Birling in "An Inspector Calls" by J. B. Priestly, for instance, did not care about Eva Smith's life outside the factory, because he knew that nobody would hold him responsible for firing her.

i. **Share with the class.**

137. ACTIVITY–WRITE AN ARGUMENTATIVE ESSAY

In her novel "The Awakening," Kate Chopin tells us that Mrs. Pontellier realized from an early age "the dual life - that outward existence which conforms, the inward life which questions." In his famous essay "Self-Reliance," Ralph Waldo Emerson declares: "What I must do is all that concerns me, not what the people think. It is easy in the world to live after the world's opinion, it is easy in solitude to live after our own." In his essay "How to Make the Best of Life," Samuel Butler declares that "Life is like playing a violin solo in public and learning the instrument as one goes on. The question is [...] the life we know, or the life which others may know, but which we know not?" Emerson believes that conformity is the death of an authentic life, and that we should never rely on other people's judgments and opinions. Samuel Butler points out that for many people, death is not the end of life, and that they live on through something enduring they created for the benefit of all.

Consider these questions in your writing. Discuss them in groups first.

1. Is life without conformity possible?
2. Where should we look for the truth?
3. Does living for others offer a better life than living for oneself?
4. What is the difference between inward and outward truth? Which one is more important?
5. Can social limitations offer more benefits than problems?
6. Is life outside community life possible? If yes, can it be a happy life?
7. What are the causes of envy?
8. What are the causes of imitation?
9. What are the results of imitation?
10. How does conformity provide safety?
11. Is it wrong to wish safety rather than authenticity?
12. Can we always trust our own mind?
13. Is being true to yourself no matter what an admirable pursuit?

Write an argumentative essay.

Argue *for or against social conformity*. Follow the guiding steps provided. Feel free to add your own thoughts and ideas.

Discuss in class the following statement:

My life is my own to live as I please, and what others think of me is none of my concern.

Include these questions in your discussion.

1. What is social conformity?
2. What is social nonconformity?
3. How important is social conformity for the wellbeing of the individual?
4. What are the implications of nonconformity?
5. Name at least two reasons why *we should care or not* about others' opinions of us (which you are going to argue for in your essay)

ORGANIZE YOUR IDEAS

a. Write an introduction in which you include ideas from your previous discussions.

b. Write the first body paragraph in which you discuss one reason why we should care *or* not about what others think of us.

c. Write the second body paragraph in which you discuss another reason why we should concern ourselves *or* not about what others think of us.

d. Write the third body paragraph in which you refer to an opposite view. In other words, if you believe *there is no point in concerning ourselves* with what others think of us, discuss why some people might disagree with you. If you believe *it is vital to have regard for* others' opinions of us, discuss why others might disagree with you.

e. Write a concluding paragraph in which you summarize ideas. Write some final thoughts.

PHRASES AND IDEAS BANK
The need to fit in is the strongest human need.
Conformity diminishes the feelings of anxiety and increases the feelings of safety.
All social behavior is determined by the desire to be accepted and valued.
Nonconformity is often followed by isolation and humiliation.
Rebelliousness makes you feel you have control of your life, and not merely live up to others' expectations.
Imitating others is important for our survival as social beings.
Being nonconformist can alienate your family, friends and coworkers.

138. ACTIVITY—WRITE AN ARGUMENTATIVE ESSAY

There is hardly a person in the world who has never experienced regret, a feeling of disappointment or sadness over things we have done or left undone. We all have experienced the wish that things were different than they actually are. Regret is also closely associated with guilt and shame, and it is generally considered a useless emotion. It is the emotion that nags at us with potential scenarios of actions and outcomes, *what if, if only, I should have, I could have*. As English essayist Arthur Christopher Benson puts it, "It is no exaggeration to say that the greater part of human happiness and unhappiness consists in the dwelling upon what has been, what may be, what might be, and, alas, in our worst moments, upon what might have been." But this nagging feeling also has the moral function of making us reevaluate our past. Regret essentially urges us to make a moral evaluation of our past conduct. It asks us to look back at the choices we made or failed to make, and assess their impact on both our own present and that of others.

Consider these questions in your writing. Discuss them in groups first.

1. Can you change future behavior if you do not regret past mistakes?
2. What is the relation between regret and moral behavior?
3. What is the relation between pain and discomfort?
4. Should we avoid or embrace pain and discomfort?
5. How does regret make us embrace our own imperfection as well as that of others?
6. Are we the same as we were a few years or even months ago? How can you connect this to regret?
7. Is there any use in ruminating about the past when life is about moving towards the future?

Write an argumentative essay in which you discuss the *usefulness or uselessness* of regret. Follow the guiding steps provided. Feel free to add your own thoughts and ideas.

Discuss the statement below in class.

Regret is a waste of time; there is no point in being sorry for something you can do nothing about.

Consider these questions in your discusson.

1. When do we feel regret and why?
2. What does regret make us think and do?
3. Is life without regret possible?
4. Does regret do us a service or disservice?
5. Name at least two benefits or downsides of regret (which you are going to argue for in your essay)

ORGANIZE YOUR IDEAS

a. Write an introduction in which you include ideas from your previous discussions.

b. Write the first body paragraph in which you discuss one benefit *or* downside of regret.

c. Write the second body paragraph in which you discuss another advantage *or* disadvantage of regret.

d. Write the third body paragraph in which you refer to an opposite view of regret. In other words, if you believe regret is *useful*, discuss why some people might disagree with you. If you believe regret is *useless*, discuss why others might disagree with you.

e. Write a concluding paragraph in which you summarize ideas. Write some final thoughts.

PHRASES AND IDEAS BANK

Regret constitutes continuous moral rebalancing between our individuality and the world around us.
Regret is a venture into something that is highly irrational and maladaptive.
Any feeling of regret is bound to have a degree of self-awareness.
An evaluation of past conduct results in changed behavior in the future.
Regret provides us with the possibility to envisage all kinds of possible scenarios in which things would have been different.
Dwelling on the past is not going to enliven our spirit.
A rational being does not let the emotional side be in control of reason.
No feelings should be wasted on things that could not be remediated or retrieved for improvement.

PRACTICE WRITING ARGUMENTATIVE ESSAYS

As mentioned earlier in the book, most tasks on tests and exams require that you offer evidence in your essays. Every time you make a claim, you should offer evidence relevant to the issue you are discussing. The following activities are meant to help you practice writing by offering guidelines and subject relevant material to organize your essays.

RELEVANT TEXTS AND FILMS for the activities that follow:

SHORT STORIES

"A Cup of Tea" by Katherine Mansfield
"The Story of an Hour" by Kate Chopin
"The Yellow Wallpaper" by Charlotte Perkins Gilman
"New Directions" by Maya Angelou
"The Doll's House" by Katherine Mansfield
"The Garden Party" by Katherine Mansfield
"Sweetness" by Toni Morrison
"Desiree's Baby" by Kate Chopin
"Going Home" by Pete Hamill
"Thank you, Ma'am" by Langston Hughes
"The Birthmark" by Nathaniel Hawthorne
"A Pair of Silk Stockings" by Kate Chopin
"The Gift of the Magi" by O. Henry

POEMS

"Still I Rise" by Maya Angelou
"Mirror" by Sylvia Plath

PLAY

"An Inspector Calls" by J. B. Priestly

FILMS

"Selma" (2014 Drama/History)
"Iron Jawed Angels" (2004 Docudrama)
"Dead Poets Society" (1989 Drama)
"Into the Wild" (2007 Biographical Drama)
"Crash" (2004 Drama)
"The Pursuit of Happyness" (2006)
"A Raisin in the Sun" (2008)
"An Inspector Calls" (2015)

139. ACTIVITY—WRITE AN ARGUMENTIVE ESSAY

In groups, discuss the statement below.

Sometimes, forgiving is the same as encouraging people to make the same mistake again.

Include the questions below in your discussion. Write an introduction by including some of the ideas you have discussed.

> **RELEVANT STORIES**
>
> "Going Home" by Pete Hamill
>
> "Thank you, Ma'am" by Langston Hughes

1. What is forgiveness?
2. What is easy to forgive?
3. What is hard to forgive?
4. Does forgiveness have more advantages or disadvantages?
5. Name two most important advantages or disadvantages.

a. **Write the first body paragraph.**

In the short story "Going Home," Vingo is forgiven by his wife but we are never told about his wrongdoing, and we do not know his wife's reasons for forgiving him. Vingo himself is anxious and not sure whether he is going to be forgiven. Write a paragraph in which you speculate about possible wrongdoings Vingo might have done and whether it was right to forgive him.

b. **Write the second body paragraph.**

In the short story "Thank you, Ma'am," Mrs. Luella takes Roger home and gives him food and money instead of turning him in. She decides to teach him a lesson by forgiving him. Write a paragraph in which you argue whether her decision was wise or unwise.

c. **Write the third body paragraph.**

Write a paragraph in which you discuss a counterargument to your previous thoughts and ideas. If you disagree with the statement, reflect on why some people might agree with it. If you agree with the statement, consider why others might disagree.

d. **Write a concluding paragraph in which you summarize ideas. Write some final thoughts.**

Consider these questions in your writing. Discuss them in groups.

1. Is it always right to forgive?
2. Do we ever learn from our mistakes if we are easily forgiven?
3. What are the benefits of anger?
4. Is it right to forgive someone who does not repent?
5. Does blame have any value?
6. Do people ever change completely?
7. Are there things which should never be forgiven?
8. What are the consequences of never forgiving?
9. What are the consequences of never being forgiven?

140. ACTIVITY–WRITE AN ARGUMENTATIVE ESSAY

Racial prejudice, its power and devastating consequences are major themes in Kate Chopin's short story "Desiree's Baby" and Toni Morrison's short story "Sweetness". By reading the stories, we witness the brutality of prejudicial attitudes and behavior, which do not spare even the most fundamental relationships humans have, the one between husband and wife, and mother and daughter.

> **RELEVANT TEXTS**
> "Sweetness"
> by Toni Morrison
> "Desiree's Baby"
> by Kate Chopin

In groups, discuss the statement below.

Prejudice and the need for social approval very often go hand in hand. In fact, literature shows that prejudice can be more powerful than love.

Include the questions below in your discussion. Write an introduction by including some of the ideas you have discussed.

1. How are prejudices formed?
2. What are the causes and implications of racism?
3. Are people mainly victims or perpetrators of racism?
4. Name the reason(s) why prejudice can be more powerful than love.

a. **Write the first body paragraph.**

In the short story "Sweetness," the narrator tells us about her relationship with her daughter. In the story, we witness the cruelty of racial prejudice and how it affects even the most elemental human relationship. Prejudice proves to be stronger than love. Write a paragraph in which you discuss how prejudice overshadows love in the story.

> **Consider these questions. Discuss them in groups.**
>
> 1. How do we know that Sweetness regards social status as more important than the happiness of her own family?
> 2. Is Sweetness justified in her decision to distance herself from her daughter?
> 3. What are the skin privileges she believes society offers/denies?
> 4. Does Sweetness try to make a change in the world or is she only perpetuating a world of injustice?
> 5. Did Sweetness live a fulfilling life? What could have been the alternative?

b. **Write the second body paragraph.**

In the short story "Desiree's Baby," Armand renounces his feelings for Desiree and his baby when he inculpates her of having black blood. In the story, we witness the brutality of racial prejudice and how it affects even the most elemental relationships. Prejudice proves to be stronger than love. Write a paragraph in which you discuss how prejudice overshadows love in the story.

> **Consider these questions. Discuss in groups.**
>
> 1. What are Armand's feelings for Desiree before the baby is born?
> 2. Why and how do his feelings change after the baby was born?
> 3. What is he afraid of losing when he suspects that Desiree has black blood?
> 4. What is he willing to sacrifice his happiness for?
> 5. Is Armand's cruelty against his wife justified?

c. **Write the third body paragraph.**

"Sweetness" was published in "The New Yorker" in 2015, while "Desiree's Baby" was published in "Vogue" in 1893. However, racial prejudice and its disturbing effects have not changed drastically from the nineteenth century south to the twenty first century America. Write a paragraph in which you discuss *the similar consequences* of prejudice in the two stories.

d. **Write a concluding paragraph. Summarize the main ideas discussed in the essay. Write some final thoughts.**

141. ACTIVITY – WRITE AN ARGUMENTIVE ESSAY

Freedom, oppression, repression, and a lack of self-awareness are some of the central themes that "The Story of an Hour" and "The Yellow Wallpaper" deal with. The female protagonists find themselves trapped in a web of emotional confusion and intellectual helplessness caused by a male-dominated world.

> **RELEVANT TEXTS**
>
> "The Story of an Hour" by Kate Chopin
>
> "The Yellow Wallpaper" by Charlotte Perkins Gilman
>
> "Mirror" by Sylvia Plath

In groups, discuss the statement below.

Freedom and self-knowledge are inseparable phenomena.

Include the questions below in your discussion. Write an introduction by including some of the ideas you have discussed.

1. Can you know yourself when you are not free?
2. Do we always know when we are not free?
3. How does lack of freedom impede self-knowledge?

a. Write the first body paragraph.

In the short story "The Story of an Hour", the protagonist finds out that her husband has been in a fatal accident. Of course, her first reaction is of deep grief. However, alone in her room, contemplating her future life, she finds herself taken over by an exalting feeling of relief. Life turns suddenly from being a burden into a promising land of unexplored treasures. Write a paragraph in which you speculate about the reasons why she was unaware of her real feelings, and how a lack of freedom meant a lack of desire to live a long life.

b. Write the second body paragraph.

In the short story "The Yellow Wallpaper", the narrator tells us of her life which is nothing more than a prison. She doubts the reasons of her being isolated in a room (with depressing yellow wallpaper), but still trusts her husband having the best intentions when he insists that this is the only way for her to get better. Her husband (and her brother) tell her that the only way for her to eradicate her depression and anxiety is to lie in bed and rest. Write a paragraph in which you discuss how the narrator's husband controls her mind and body, thus hindering her from finding out what she really feels and thinks about herself and her life.

c. Write the third body paragraph.

In her poem "Mirror", Sylvia Plath points to the tension women often feel between their outer and inner selves. Social conventions and expectations are often in conflict with inner desires and emotions. Write a paragraph in which you discuss the challenges women struggle with when they try to reconcile their inner yearnings with their external demands.

d. Write a concluding paragraph. Summarize the main ideas discussed in the essay. Write some final thoughts.

> **Consider these questions in your writing. Discuss them in groups or class.**
>
> 1. When do we have doubts about who we really are?
> 2. Are we the reflected image we get from others?
> 3. Are we what others expect us to be?
> 4. Was freedom and marriage always in harmony with each other in the past?
> 5. Is/was marriage different for men and for women?
> 6. What are the consequences of repression?
> 7. What are the consequences of self-repression?
> 8. Is a woman's happiness or unhappiness directly related to the presence of a man?

142. ACTIVITY–WRITE AN ARGUMENTATIVE ESSAY

The American Dream is based on the belief that if you work hard enough, you can get the life you want. If you believe in yourself, nothing is impossible. Regardless of where you come from, you are given an equal chance to succeed. However, as history and fiction reveal, this is not true for everyone. Success and happiness depend on many other factors beside hard work.

> **RELEVANT FILMS**
>
> "The Pursuit of Happyness"
> "A Raisin in the Sun"

In groups, discuss the statement below.

The American Dream remains only a dream for some.

Include the questions below in your discussion. Write an introduction by including some of the ideas you have discussed.

1. What is the American Dream?
2. Is it attainable for everyone?
3. What is the difference between *pursuing* happiness and *achieving* it?
4. Can hard work alone make our dreams come true? Refer to the two films in your answer.

a. Write the first body paragraph.

The film "The Pursuit of Happyness" deals with the American Dream among other themes. Write a paragraph in which you discuss the film's perspective on the American Dream. Focus on perseverance and money as essential factors which influence its attainment.

> **Consider these questions. Discuss them in groups.**
>
> 1. What is the American Dream for Chris?
> 2. What is the role of luck in Chris's happiness?
> 3. What is the role of money in measuring his happiness?
> 4. Does Chris make his own opportunities or does he wait for others to offer them to him?
> 5. What is the role of perseverance in making his American Dream attainable?

b. Write the second body paragraph.

The film "A Raisin in the Sun," based on Lorraine Hansberry's play with the same name, deals among other things with the American Dream. Write a paragraph in which you discuss the film's (play's) perspective on the American Dream. Focus on racial and gender prejudices, opportunity and perseverance as essential factors which influence its attainment.

> **Consider these questions. Discuss them in groups.**
>
> 1. What is the American Dream for Walter?
> 2. What is the role of circumstances in Walter's happiness?
> 3. What is the role of money in measuring his happiness?
> 4. Does Walter make his own opportunities or does he wait for others to offer them to him?
> 5. What is the role of perseverance in making his American Dream attainable?

    c. **Write the third body paragraph.**

"The Pursuit of Happyness" and "A Raisin in the Sun" deal with the challenges people face in their pursuit of the American Dream. Write a paragraph in which you focus on the differences (and/or similarities if you believe there are any) of these challenges in the two stories.

    d. **Write a concluding paragraph. Summarize the main ideas discussed in the essay.**

143. ACTIVITY – WRITE AN ARGUMENTIVE ESSAY

Inequality, injustice, and prejudice are only some of the themes that "Selma" and "Iron Jawed Angels" deal with. They tell us stories of people who risked their lives and faced harsh consequences by demanding justice and equality for all.

> **RELEVANT FILMS**
> "Selma"
> "Iron Jawed Angels"

In groups, discuss the statement below.

It takes courage and personal sacrifice to fight for equality and justice for all.

Include the questions below in your discussion. Write an introduction by including some of the ideas you have discussed.

1. When do we identify injustice and inequality?
2. What are the ways to fight injustice?
3. What makes people risk their lives for the common good?

a. Write the first body paragraph.

Write a paragraph in which you discuss *courage* as an essential element in the fight against racial and gender inequality throughout history. Offer examples of courage as a pervasive quality in the films (and/or texts you read online).

b. Write the second body paragraph.

Write a paragraph in which you discuss *personal sacrifice* as an essential element in the fight against racial and gender inequality throughout history. Offer examples of personal sacrifice as a pervasive quality in the films (and/or texts you read online).

c. Write the third body paragraph.

Write a paragraph in which you discuss the significance of fearless and determined people who are willing to dedicate their lives for a more just society.

d. Write a concluding paragraph. Summarize the main ideas discussed in your essay. Write some final thoughts.

Consider these questions in your writing. Discuss them in groups or class.

1. What cements injustice and inequality?
2. What makes the fight against racial inequality so hard?
3. What makes the fight against gender inequality so hard?
4. Is courage something we can learn and practice?
5. When does personal sacrifice become necessary?
6. What other qualities ensue when you have the courage to stand for what you believe in?
7. How can prejudiced attitudes and behaviors be eradicated?
8. Why is it important to look back in history and remember people who fought for equal rights?
9. How can we make ourselves remember to never take our welfare for granted?

144. ACTIVITY- WRITE AN ARGUMENTATIVE ESSAY

The play "An Inspector Calls" by J. B. Priestly and the short story "A Cup of Tea" by Katherine Mansfield deal with social consciousness, the upper class's feelings of entitlement and superiority, as well as their views of the poor as creatures to use for their benefit or entertainment.

> RELEVANT TEXTS
> "An Inspector Calls" by J. B. Priestly
> "A Cup of Tea" by Katherine Mansfield

In groups, discuss the statement below.

Literature shows us how the rich live in a world of privileges that protect them from the harsh realities of life. This also makes them believe they are entitled to it.

Write an introduction. (Suggestion: you might try to leave your introduction to the end)

a. Write the first body paragraph.

In the play "An Inspector Calls," we are introduced to several characters who belong to the upper class. Each of them seems to have very little understanding of what it means to be poor. Eva Smith, a representative of the struggling working class, is a far-off creature for whom they have no compassion nor understanding. Write a paragraph in which you discuss how Gerald's and the Birlings' thoughts and behaviors reveal the distance between the rich and the poor.

b. Write the second body paragraph.

In the short story "A Cup of Tea," Rosemary Fell seems clueless of a world in which people have no money for a cup of tea. For her, this sounds like something taken out of a book by Dostoyevsky. When she meets the poor hungry girl, her immediate thoughts are of how adventurous this could be and takes her home, where she orders brandy rather than food. Write a paragraph in which you discuss how Rosemary's thoughts and behavior reveal the distance between the rich and the poor.

c. Write the third body paragraph.

"A Cup of Tea" was published in "The Story-Teller" in 1922, and "An Inspector Calls" was published in 1945. Both stories deal with social class and the discrepancy between the lifestyles and worldviews of the rich and the poor. Write a paragraph in which you discuss the similarities between these worldviews in the two stories.

d. Write a concluding paragraph. Summarize the main ideas discussed in the essay.

145. ACTIVITY–WRITE AN ARGUMENTATIVE ESSAY

a. **In groups, discuss the question below.**

Should we live life with passion or with caution?

> **RELEVANT FILMS**
> "Dead Poets Society"
> "Into the Wild"

Include the questions below in your discussion.

1. What does it mean to live with passion?
2. What does it mean to live with caution?
3. Which is the best: the cautious or the passionate life? Give at least three reasons. Offer examples to illustrate them.

b. **Write an argumentative essay in which you discuss and reflect on the question. Follow the outline below. Follow the first body paragraph when you write the other two.**

INTRODUCTION
Introduce your claim, which is one of the two below. Name your reasons.

1. We should live our life with passion.
2. It is better to live cautiously rather than passionately.

BODY PARAGRAPH 1
- **Point**
  Passion makes us live an authentic life and be true to ourselves.
- **Evidence**
  In the movie "Into the Wild", Chris chose his own path and the way he wanted to live. He took the less travelled way.
- **Explanation**
  Chris was not afraid of taking the risk of living in different places alone and away from his family to follow his dreams. He was proud that he got the chance to do what he wanted. His death was an accident that could have happened in a normal life to anyone. The risk he took was not the main reason of his death.

BODY PARAGRAPH 2
Second point, Evidence, Explanations
BODY PARAGRAPH 3
Second point, Evidence, Explanations
CONCLUSION
Reiterate main points. Summarize ideas.

146. ACTIVITY–WRITE AN ARGUMENTATIVE ESSAY

a. **In groups, discuss the statement below.**

In class societies, people are less concerned with the wellbeing of others.

Include the questions below in your discussion.

> **RELEVANT TEXTS**
> "The Doll's House" by Katherine Mansfield
> "The Garden Party" by Katherine Mansfield
> "A Cup of Tea" by Katherine Mansfield
> "An Inspector Calls" by J. B. Priestly

1. How and why do people express compassion?
2. Describe and give examples of relations between the rich and the poor.
3. What makes people unconcerned with others' welfare?

b. **Write an argumentative essay in which you discuss the statement above. Follow the outline below. Follow the first body paragraph when you write the other two body paragraphs.**

INTRODUCTION
Introduce your claim, and name your reasons.

BODY PARAGRAPH 1
- **Point**
  In class societies, the distance between different classes makes them less empathetic with others.
- **Evidence**
  For example, in the short story "A Cup of Tea", Rosemary does not understand the poor girl's hunger and exhaustion because the situation is foreign to her. She offers the almost fainting girl brandy instead of food.
- **Explanation**
  This shows how Rosemary's lack of empathy is due to her lack of understanding. Because she never has contact with the working class, she does not know what it means to be poor. To not be able to afford a cup of tea is beyond her imagination. It is hard for people to care about other people's wellbeing when the economic and social distance between them is immense.

BODY PARAGRAPH 2 Second point, Evidence, Explanations
BODY PARAGRAPH 3 Second point, Evidence, Explanations
CONCLUSION Reiterate main points. Summarize ideas.

147. ACTIVITY–WRITE AN ARGUMENTATIVE ESSAY

> **RELEVANT TEXT**
> "New Directions" by Maya Angelou

a. In groups, discuss the statement below.

It is never too late to change directions.

Include the following questions in your discussion.

In "New Directions", Maya Angelou writes:
Each of us has the right and the responsibility to assess the roads which lie ahead, and those over which we have traveled, and if the future road looms ominous or unpromising, and the roads back uninviting, then we need to gather our resolve and, carrying only the necessary baggage, step off that road into another direction. If the new choice is also unpalatable, without embarrassment, we must be ready to change that as well.

1. What is the difference between right and responsibility in this context?
2. When do we feel that the future road seems worrying?
3. Is there a right time for giving up?
4. Is there a wrong time to make a change?
5. Is age a hinder or an advantage to change?

b. Write an argumentative essay in which you comment on the statement above.

> **INTRODUCTION**
> Introduce your claim, and name your reasons.
>
> **BODY PARAGRAPH 1**
> - Point
> - Evidence
> - Explanation
>
> **BODY PARAGRAPH 2**
> Second point, Evidence, Explanations
> **BODY PARAGRAPH 3**
> Second point, Evidence, Explanations
> **CONCLUSION**
> Reiterate main points. Summarize ideas.

148. ACTIVITY–WRITE AN ARGUMENTATIVE ESSAY

> **RELEVANT TEXT**
> "A Pair of Silk Stockings" by Kate Chopin

a. In groups, discuss the statement below.

Sometimes, personal satisfaction should precede family responsibilities.

Include the following questions in your discussion.

1. When and why do we make sacrifices?
2. Why should everybody indulge themselves sometimes?
3. Is being a woman different from being a mother and wife?
4. What is more important when you are a mother and a wife?
5. Are there pleasures that only money can buy?

b. Write an argumentative essay in which you comment on the statement above.

> **INTRODUCTION**
> Introduce your claim, and name your reasons.
>
> **BODY PARAGRAPH 1**
> - Point
> - Evidence
> - Explanation
>
> **BODY PARAGRAPH 2**
> Second point, Evidence, Explanations
> **BODY PARAGRAPH 3**
> Second point, Evidence, Explanations
> **CONCLUSION**
> Reiterate main points. Summarize ideas.

149. ACTIVITY—WRITE AN ARGUMENTATIVE ESSAY

> **RELEVANT TEXT**
> "The Birthmark" by Nathaniel Hawthorne

a. **In groups, discuss the statement below.**

Self-sacrifice is an essential part of all romantic relationships.

Include the following questions in your discussion.

1. Is it natural for people to want to fix their physical imperfections?
2. Is an endless search for perfection a good thing?
3. Do we all want a perfect partner?
4. Should we accept our partners to criticize our physical imperfections?

b. **Write an argumentative essay in which you agree or disagree with the statement above.**

> **INTRODUCTION**
> Introduce your claim, and name your reasons.
>
> **BODY PARAGRAPH 1**
> - Point
> - Evidence
> - Explanation
>
> **BODY PARAGRAPH 2**
> Second point, Evidence, Explanations
> **BODY PARAGRAPH 3**
> Second point, Evidence, Explanations
> **CONCLUSION**
> Reiterate main points. Summarize ideas.

150. ACTIVITY–WRITE AN ARGUMENTATIVE ESSAY

a. **In groups, discuss the statement below.**

Literature and films are not merely sources of entertainment.
They are in fact great sources of learning.

b. **Write an argumentative essay in which you discuss and reflect on how literature and films teach us valuable lessons. Follow the outline below.**

INTRODUCTION	What are some of the most important lessons literature and films teach us? Name three of them (which you will discuss in your three body paragraphs).
BODY PARAGRAPH 1 First point Evidence Explanations	Topic sentence: *To begin with, we learn from films that we should not give up if we want to achieve our dreams.*
BODY PARAGRAPH 2 Second point Evidence Explanations	Topic sentence: *Furthermore, films teach us that social and political change requires personal sacrifice.*
BODY PARAGRAPH 3 Third point Evidence Explanations	Topic sentence: *Ultimately, we learn that many social issues cannot be resolved by only one person, and that people need to stand and work together in their fight for a cause.*
CONCLUSION	Restate the main lessons you have discussed. Write some final thoughts.

PRACTICE WRITING COMPARISON ESSAYS

In this section, you will practice writing comparison essays. As you remember, comparison essays can be organized subject by subject, or point by point.

151. ACTIVITY—WRITE A COMPARISON ESSAY

RELEVANT FILMS
"Dead Poets Society"
"Into the Wild"

Write an essay in which you compare the two protagonists in the films "Dead Poets Society" and "Into the Wild".

The aspects below are only suggestions.

SUBJECT BY SUBJECT

The main characters in "Dead Poets Society" and "Into the Wild" are both young, passionate, and rebellious.

a. **Neil**
  1. Family background
  2. Personality
  3. Interests and dreams

b. **Chris**
  1. Family background
  2. Personality
  3. Interests and dreams

POINT BY POINT

The main characters in "Dead Poets Society" and "Into the Wild" are both young, passionate, and rebellious.

a. **Family background**
  1. Neil
  2. Chris

b. **Personality**
  1. Neil
  2. Chris

c. **Interests and dreams**
  1. Neil
  2. Chris

152. ACTIVITY–WRITE A COMPARISON ESSAY

RELEVANT TEXTS
"A Pair of Silk Stockings" by Kate Chopin
"The Gift of the Magi" by O. Henry

Write a comparison essay in which you compare the protagonists in the short stories "A Pair of Silk Stockings" and "The Gift of the Magi".

The aspects below are only suggestions.

SUBJECT BY SUBJECT

"A Pair of Silk Stockings" and "The Gift of the Magi" deal with the themes of financial scarcity and self-sacrifice.

a. **Mrs. Sommers**
   1. Family life
   2. How she spends her money

b. **Della**
   1. Family background
   2. How she spends her money

POINT BY POINT

"A Pair of Silk Stockings" and "The Gift of the Magi" deal with the themes of financial scarcity and self-sacrifice.

a. **Family life**
   1. Mrs. Sommers
   2. Della

b. **How they spend their money**
   1. Mrs. Sommers
   2. Della

153. ACTIVITY–WRITE A COMPARISON ESSAY

RELEVANT TEXTS
"The Birthmark" by Nathaniel Hawthorne
"The Gift of the Magi" by O. Henry

Write an essay in which you compare the protagonists in the short stories "The Birthmark" and "The Gift of the Magi".

The aspects below are only suggestions.

SUBJECT BY SUBJECT

Both "The Birthmark" and "The Gift of the Magi" deal with the themes of self-sacrifice for one's partner.

a. **Georgiana**
   1. Physical appearance and relationship with her husband
   2. What she sacrifices and why

b. **Della**
   1. Physical appearance and relationship with her husband
   2. What she sacrifices and why

POINT BY POINT

Both "The Birthmark" and "The Gift of the Magi" deal with the themes of self-sacrifice for one's partner.

a. **Physical appearance and relationship with her husband**
   1. Georgiana
   2. Della

b. **What they sacrifice and why**
   1. Georgiana
   2. Della

154. ACTIVITY—WRITE A COMPARISON ESSAY

> **RELEVANT FILMS**
> "The Pursuit of Happyness"
> "A Raisin in the Sun"

Write an essay in which you compare the protagonists in the films "The Pursuit of Happyness" and "A Raisin in the Sun".

The aspects below are only suggestions.

SUBJECT BY SUBJECT

Both Chris and Walter try to achieve the American Dream, but in different ways.

a. **Chris**
   1. Personality
   2. His struggles to achieve success
   3. His achievements

b. **Walter**
   1. Personality
   2. His struggles to achieve success
   3. His achievements

POINT BY POINT

Both Chris and Walter try to achieve the American Dream, but in different ways.

a. **Personality**
   1. Chris
   2. Walter

b. **Struggles**
   1. Chris
   2. Walter

c. **Achievements**
   1. Chris
   2. Walter

155. ACTIVITY–WRITE A COMPARISON ESSAY

> **RELEVANT TEXTS**
> "The Doll's House" by Katherine Mansfield
> "The Garden Party" by Katherine Mansfield

Write an essay in which you compare Kezia and Laura in the short stories "The Doll's House" and "The Garden Party".

The aspects below are only suggestions.

SUBJECT BY SUBJECT

Both Kezia in "The Doll's House" and Laura in "The Garden Party" are different from the rest of their families.

a. **Kezia**
   1. Family background
   2. Her attitudes towards the lower class
   3. How she differs from the rest of the family

b. **Laura**
   1. Family background
   2. Her attitudes towards the lower class
   3. How she differs from the rest of the family

POINT BY POINT

Both Kezia in "The Doll's House" and Laura in "The Garden Party" are different from the rest of their families.

a. **Family background**
   1. Kezia
   2. Laura

b. **Attitudes towards the poor**
   1. Kezia
   2. Laura

c. **How they differ from the rest of their families**
   1. Kezia
   2. Laura

156. ACTIVITY—WRITE A COMPARISON ESSAY

> **RELEVANT TEXT**
> "An Inspector Calls" By J. B. Priestly

Write an essay in which you compare Mr. Birling and Inspector Goole in "An Inspector Calls".

The aspects below are only suggestions.

SUBJECT BY SUBJECT

Mr. Birling and Inspector Goole have different personalities and views of social responsibility.

a. **Mr. Birling**
   1. Personality
   2. View of social responsibility

b. **Inspector Goole**
   1. Personality
   2. View of social responsibility

POINT BY POINT

Mr. Birling and Inspector Goole have different personalities and views of social responsibility.

a. **Personality**
   1. Mr. Birling
   2. Inspector Goole

b. **View of social responsibility**
   1. Mr. Birling
   2. Inspector Goole

157. ACTIVITY—WRITE A COMPARISON ESSAY

Social media has made communication across cultures and nations easier than ever before. Reading and writing are no longer activities available to the few. Everyone can read almost everything that has ever been written, and anyone can become a writer should they feel they have something of importance to communicate to the world. Social media include web-pages and applications which offer platforms of social networking, such as Facebook, Twitter, Instagram, blogs, discussion forums, etc. Traditional media refer to mass communication forms such as television, radio, newspapers, magazines, and other print publications.

Use the block method to write an essay in which you compare social media with traditional media. Follow the guiding steps provided. Feel free to add your own thoughts and ideas.

a. **Write an introduction to your essay.**

Include these aspects:

- When and why do we use social media?
- When and why do we use traditional media?
- What makes social media necessary?
- What makes traditional media necessary?

b. **Write the first body paragraph in which you discuss the benefits of social media.**

Consider these aspects:

- You keep in touch with old and current friends, and are updated on what goes on around the world.
- You get a better understanding and can be active in debates and discussions on important social issues.
- You can engage in exchanges of opinions and views with like-minded people, as well as people with different views from your own.
- The world presents itself in a broader and more nuanced way, and you have the freedom to choose your own content and medium of information communication.

c. Write the second body paragraph in which you discuss the problems of social media.

Consider these aspects:

- It is challenging to separate fact from fiction, and truth from pretense.
- People become more anxious and insecure because they compare themselves with others, and chase ideals which are not necessarily realistic.
- It is easy to choose the platforms that share your own views, and thus avoid challenging yourself with new perspectives and interpretations.
- You are exposed to unkind and unfair personal criticism or even hate speech.

d. Write the third body paragraph in which you discuss the benefits of traditional media.

Consider these aspects:

- You get authentic and reliable accounts of events.
- Everybody can relate to the same events and information, which creates a stronger feeling of community life.
- You get high-quality analysis and discussions, which also provide the masses with knowledge-based broadcasting.
- Traditional media create a feeling of trust within traditional institutions and strengthens cultural belonging.

e. Write the fourth body paragraph in which you discuss the limitations of traditional media.

Consider these aspects:

- We are passive receivers of polished content, as it is a one-way communication form.
- Traditional media are limiting in terms of economic and timely availability.
- They offer partial presentation and interpretation of events and ideas.
- Traditional media entail a lack of choice of content and manner of communication.

f. Write a concluding paragraph. Summarize the main ideas discussed in the essay. Write some final thoughts.

g. Compare your essays in groups.

REFLECT. SHARE. WRITE.

In this last section of the book, you will be offered questions for reflection. They are meant to guide you in your writing and to offer you the opportunity to make your thoughts and life experiences meaningful.

One of the most important elements of learning is reflecting over the meaning of things. Indeed, the point of all learning is to improve our lives, and we do that by creating a coherent and meaningful understanding of the world around us. But understanding the world entails understanding ourselves too. And even if it might seem like a given that we know ourselves better than anyone, self-knowledge is one of the hardest things to achieve. Every day we are exposed to myriads of experiences and impressions which form our identity. But we rarely sit down and reflect over their significance and impact on who we are or become.

Writing reflective essays can be a great opportunity to cogitate on the nature of your experiences and their influence on you. It offers the occasion to understand the world and your place in it. A reflective essay, unlike other types of essays, is a highly personal text. It does not always need to be backed up by evidence, but it does acquire more substance when anchored in real life events and experiences. Most importantly, though, a reflective essay is meant to create meaning and express the essence of things.

Each activity is based on one concept. You may use the questions to guide your writing later, but you are encouraged to discuss them with your classmates. In this way, you will get insight not only in your own understanding, but others' as well.

NB! No questions should be answered with *yes* or *no*. You should always explain why your answer is positive or negative – give reasons for your view.

158. ACTIVITY—REFLECT AND WRITE ABOUT TALENT

A. What is talent?

1. What can you do easily and well?
2. How is talent different from skill?
3. Can a person turn a skill into a talent?
4. Is talent inborn or learned?
5. Is talent knowledge or practice?

B. How is talent discovered?

1. What is the link between talent and luck?
2. What is the connection between talent and determination?
3. Are talented people better learners?
4. What is the link between talent and environment?
5. Who is responsible for discovering our talents?

C. Do we always know our talents?

1. How do people discover their talents?
2. How can people waste their talents?
3. What is the link between self-knowledge and talent?
4. Is it possible to be talented and not know it?
5. Is it possible to have no talents at all?

D. Is being talented the same as successful?

1. What makes a person successful?
2. How is a talented person different from an untalented one?
3. What is the relation between talent and fame?
4. Is being good at something the same as being talented?
5. Is being good at something enough to feel fulfilled?

A. Write an introduction in which you define talent.
B. Write a paragraph in which you discuss how circumstances help us discover our talent(s).
C. Write a paragraph in which you discuss how discovering your talent depends on self-knowledge.
D. Write a paragraph in which you discuss whether talent has anything to do with success or happiness.
E. Write a conclusion in which you sum up your ideas.

159. ACTIVITY–REFLECT AND WRITE ABOUT CURIOSITY

A. What is curiosity?

1. How does a curious person behave?
2. What makes you want to know more about something?
3. Are you curious about familiar things?
4. Are you curious about unfamiliar things?
5. How do you describe a curious mind?

B. What makes you curious?

1. What attracts your attention when you read something?
2. What attracts your attention when you talk with somebody?
3. Are you interested in things that are new or old?
4. Are you curious about people?
5. Are you curious about things that are strange?

C. Is curiosity important for learning?

1. What do you find exciting to learn?
2. Are you curious about what you do not understand?
3. Do you find interesting the past or the future?
4. How does curiosity motivate us?
5. Can you learn new things without being curious?

D. Is curiosity always positive?

1. What is passion for gossip?
2. When does curiosity change into fixation?
3. When is being curious the same as being nosy?
4. Can we be curious when we are bored?
5. Can curiosity be trained?

A. Write an introduction in which you define curiosity.
B. Write a paragraph in which you reflect over the things that you find interesting.
C. Write a paragraph in which you discuss the association between curiosity and learning.
D. Write a paragraph in which you discuss some negative aspects about being curious. Or are there only positive things about being curious?
E. Write a conclusion in which you sum up your ideas.

160. ACTIVITY—REFLECT AND WRITE ABOUT DREAMS

A. What are dreams?

1. Is dreaming the same as imagining?
2. Are dreams the same as ambitions?
3. Are dreams the same as goals?
4. Do dreams show satisfaction or dissatisfaction?
5. What does *to dream big* mean?

B. Why do we dream?

1. What are dreams based on?
2. Do our dreams change or stay the same?
3. Do we dream only about the future?
4. Is dreaming the same as hoping?
5. Can we live without dreams?

C. Should we have only realistic dreams?

1. What is your concept of *a dream life*?
2. Can you be anything you want?
3. Is it beneficial to believe you can be anything you want?
4. Can dreams be predictions?
5. Do dreams generally come true?

D. Do our dreams define us?

1. Do we dream of what we know or what we don't?
2. Do we dream of what we have or what we don't?
3. Do dreams tell us what we need?
4. How do our dreams express our culture?
5. How do extract meaning from our dreams?

A. Write an introduction in which you define dreams.
B. Write a paragraph in which you reflect over what makes us have dreams.
C. Write a paragraph in which you discuss whether having unrealistic dreams is a positive thing.
D. Write a paragraph in which you discuss how our dreams are (or not) connected to who we are.
E. Write a conclusion in which you sum up your ideas.

161. ACTIVITY—REFLECT AND WRITE ABOUT CONFLICTS

A. What is a conflict?

1. When do people disagree?
2. How do people behave when they disagree?
3. When do countries disagree?
4. How do countries show their disagreements?
5. What makes a situation conflictual?

B. What causes conflicts?

1. What are common conflicts at home?
2. What are common conflicts at work?
3. What are common conflicts at school?
4. What kinds of conflicts are caused by misunderstandings?
5. What types of conflicts are produced by disagreements?

C. How do we handle conflicts?

1. How do people deal with each other's differences?
2. What makes open-mindedness important?
3. How do we change our opinions?
4. How do we become tolerant?
5. How do we learn to agree to disagree?

D. Should we avoid or face conflicts?

1. Are your needs always more important?
2. Can disagreements be beneficial?
3. Can listening instead of speaking be a solution?
4. Should we always express our feelings?
5. When is speaking up more important than keeping quiet?

A. Write an introduction in which you define conflicts.
B. Write a paragraph in which you discuss different situations causing different conflicts.
C. Write a paragraph in which you discuss different ways of dealing with conflicts.
D. Write a paragraph in which you discuss whether the best strategy to deal with conflicts is to avoid them or to face them.
E. Write a conclusion in which you sum up your ideas.

162. ACTIVITY—REFLECT AND WRITE ABOUT UNFAIRNESS

A. What is fairness?

1. Is being fair the same as just?
2. Is being fair the same as kind?
3. What makes a person unfair?
4. What makes a situation unfair?
5. Is fair the same as equal?

B. What is unfairness?

1. What is unfair treatment?
2. Can parents be unfair with their children?
3. Can children be unfair with their parents?
4. Can the law be unfair?
5. Can a society be unfair?

C. Is it easy to be fair?

1. Would you accept an unfair advantage?
2. Would you accept an unfair disadvantage?
3. How do you feel when you get less than others?
4. How do you feel when you get more than others?
5. How often do you sacrifice your needs for others?

D. Is fairness easy to recognize?

1. What is a fair relationship?
2. Is a robot fairer than a human?
3. What is an unfair offer?
4. What is a fair deal?
5. Do we always know when we are unfair?

A. Write an introduction in which you define fairness.
B. Write a paragraph in which you discuss unfair situations.
C. Write a paragraph in which you discuss the feelings caused by fairness and unfairness.
D. Write a paragraph in which you discuss whether we are always aware of being fair to others or others being fair to us.
E. Write a conclusion in which you sum up your ideas.

163. ACTIVITY–REFLECT AND WRITE ABOUT HAPPINESS

A. What is happiness?

1. How do you know when you are happy?
2. What makes you content?
3. What are you happy to do?
4. What are you happy to have?
5. What are the most important elements of happiness?

B. Is happy the same as fulfilled?

1. What are you very good at?
2. Can happiness be an activity?
3. Is being passionate about something the same as happy?
4. Do you feel happy when others need you?
5. Do you feel happy when you give or when you receive?

C. Is happiness need or desire?

1. Do you always know when you are happy?
2. Do you often wonder if you are happy?
3. Is it necessary to wonder if one is happy?
4. Is it possible to never wonder if one is happy?
5. Is happiness different at different ages?

D. Does happiness depend on us or others?

1. Should happiness be a goal?
2. Is happiness permanent?
3. Do you always know what makes you happy?
4. Are you happiest when alone or with others?
5. Is happiness a branch or the whole tree?

A. Write an introduction in which you define happiness.
B. Write a paragraph in which you discuss the connection between happiness and fulfilment.
C. Write a paragraph in which you discuss the nature of happiness.
D. Write a paragraph in which you discuss the factors your happiness depends on.
E. Write a conclusion in which you sum up your ideas.

164. ACTIVITY—REFLECT AND WRITE ABOUT FRIENDSHIP

A. What is friendship?

1. What makes you trust somebody?
2. What makes you care about somebody?
3. Is friendship based on love or respect?
4. What is the most important element in a friendship?
5. Do friends need to have common interests?

B. What is a good friend?

1. What does a good friend do for you?
2. How does a good friend make you feel?
3. Can good friends be very different from each other?
4. What makes a person accept another person unconditionally?
5. Do we always know our friends well?

C. Do we choose our friends?

1. Is friendship based on reason or feeling?
2. What is the most important quality in a friend?
3. What is the worst quality in a friend?
4. What can you easily forgive a friend?
5. What can you never forgive a friend?

D. Why do we need friends?

1. What do we usually do together with friends?
2. Is it possible to be lonely and happy?
3. Is it possible to have many friends and feel lonely?
4. Should friends accept us as we are or try to change us?
5. Should a friend make you happy or make you better?

A. Write an introduction in which you define friendship.
B. Write a paragraph in which you discuss the qualities of a good friend.
C. Write a paragraph in which you discuss the foundations of friendship.
D. Write a paragraph in which you discuss the reasons we need friends.
E. Write a conclusion in which you sum up your ideas.

165. ACTIVITY—REFLECT AND WRITE ABOUT KINDNESS

A. What is kindness?

1. What makes a person be kind?
2. Is kindness like or different from love?
3. Is kindness the same as generosity?
4. Is kindness the same as fairness?
5. Is being kind the same as being just?

B. Is it easy to be kind?

1. Are we born kind or do we learn to be kind?
2. Is it possible to be kind in all situations of life?
3. Can you be kind to somebody you dislike?
4. Can you be kind when you feel offended?
5. Is acting kindly the same as thinking kind thoughts?

C. What makes kindness pleasing?

1. Why do we think of kindness as warm?
2. Is kindness always positive?
3. Is being kind the same as being caring?
4. Is kindness wise or foolish?
5. What makes kindness contagious?

D. Is it always right to be kind?

1. Why are we unkind to others?
2. Is it right to be kind to someone who is unkind?
3. Can you ever regret being kind?
4. Is kindness the solution to all problems?
5. Is kindness more powerful than revenge?

A. Write an introduction in which you define kindness.
B. Write a paragraph in which you discuss different situations of kindness.
C. Write a paragraph in which you discuss the positive aspects of kindness.
D. Write a paragraph in which you discuss whether kindness is always the answer.
E. Write a conclusion in which you sum up your ideas.

166. ACTIVITY—REFLECT AND WRITE ABOUT POWER

A. What is power?

1. What does power make you think about?
2. What is economic power?
3. What is intellectual power?
4. What is physical power?
5. What makes somebody powerful?

B. Does everyone seek power?

1. What kinds of people love power?
2. Why do they say that history is based on the struggle for power?
3. What do countries do to obtain power in the world?
4. What do people do to obtain power in society?
5. Is there any link between self-confidence and power?

C. What makes power attractive?

1. What can you do with power?
2. What can power do to you?
3. What makes somebody powerless?
4. Is being in power the same as powerful?
5. Is being powerful the same as happy?

D. Does power always corrupt?

1. Is being powerful the same as being respected?
2. Why might people in power think they are superior?
3. What is meant by 'the power of words'?
4. How can education be power?
5. Can wisdom be power?

A. Write an introduction in which you define power.
B. Write a paragraph in which you discuss the reasons why people and countries crave power.
C. Write a paragraph about the things that make power so appealing.
D. Write a paragraph in which you discuss different kinds of power and its effects on people who hold it.
E. Write a conclusion in which you sum up your ideas.

167. ACTIVITY–REFLECT AND WRITE ABOUT RESPECT

A. What defines a respectable person?

1. What are respectable personality traits?
2. What are respectable looks?
3. What is respectable behavior?
4. Is respectable the same as loveable?
5. What is the opposite of respectable?

B. What makes you respect somebody?

1. Do you respect people who are popular?
2. Do you respect people who are successful?
3. Do you respect people very different from you?
4. Do you respect those who value wealth and fame?
5. Is respect the same as admiration?

C. Are all human relationships based on respect?

1. Why is respect important in social interactions?
2. Why is respect important at work?
3. Why is respect important at school?
4. Are relationships based on lack of respect possible?
5. Is being disrespectful ever acceptable?

D. Can you be defined by what you respect?

1. How is respect different from love?
2. What do you appreciate most in people?
3. What do you depreciate most in people?
4. Can you be unkind to someone you respect?
5. Can you be kind to someone you disrespect?

A. Write an introduction in which you discuss what makes somebody or something worthy of respect.
B. Write a paragraph in which you discuss the reasons why you respect certain people.
C. Write a paragraph in which you discuss whether respect is essential for all human relationships.
D. Write a paragraph in which you discuss your values based on who you respect.
E. Write a conclusion in which you sum up your ideas.

168. ACTIVITY–REFLECT AND WRITE ABOUT IDENTITY

A. Who are you?

1. What makes you happy?
2. What makes you sad?
3. What are you very good at?
4. What do you find interesting?
5. What do you find boring?

B. Are you your home?

1. Is home a place or a feeling?
2. Is home something you choose or something chosen for you?
3. Can home be a book, a song or a person?
4. Is it important to have a home?
5. Could you live anywhere in the world?

C. Are you your dreams?

1. What is your biggest dream?
2. What did you dream about when you were little?
3. What do you dream about now?
4. Why do dreams change?
5. Can dreams tell us who we are?

D. Who are you when nobody can see you?

1. Are you alike or different from your parents?
2. Are you alike or different from your friends?
3. What do you enjoy doing alone?
4. What do you enjoy doing with others?
5. What does happiness mean to you?

A. Write an introduction in which you discuss about the things that characterize you.
B. Write a paragraph in which you discuss what home is for you.
C. Write a paragraph in which you discuss your dreams and what they tell about who you are.
D. Write a paragraph in which you discuss who you are when there are no social constraints, when you can be and act just as you like.
E. Write a conclusion in which you sum up your ideas.

CHAPTER 1 REFERENCES

Alcott, Louisa May. 2008. *Little Women*. Urbana, Illinois: Project Gutenberg. Retrieved November 21, 2017, from www.gutenberg.org/ebooks/514. Kindle Edition.

Anderson, Sherwood. 2004. *Triumph of the Egg and Other Stories*. Urbana, Illinois: Project Gutenberg. Retrieved April 17, 2017, from www.gutenberg.org/ebooks/7048. Kindle Edition.

Baldwin, James Mark. 2007. *The Story of the Mind*. Urbana, Illinois: Project Gutenberg. Retrieved January 2, 2018, from www.gutenberg.org/ebooks/20522. Kindle Edition.

Brontë, Charlotte. 2007. *Jane Eyre: An Autobiography*. Urbana, Illinois: Project Gutenberg. Retrieved November 16, 2017, from www.gutenberg.org/ebooks/1260. Kindle Edition.

Charlotte Perkins Gilman. *The Man-Made World; Or, Our Androcentric Culture*. Urbana, Illinois: Project Gutenberg. Retrieved November 11, 2017, from www.gutenberg.org/ebooks/3015. Kindle Edition.

Chesterton, G.K. 2008. *What I saw in America*. Urbana, Illinois: Project Gutenberg. Retrieved November 25, 2017, from www.gutenberg.org/ebooks/27250. Kindle Edition.

Chopin, Kate. 2006. *The Awakening and Selected Short Stories*. Urbana, Illinois: Project Gutenberg. Retrieved January 28, 2018, from www.gutenberg.org/ebooks/160. Kindle Edition.

Chopin, Kate. 2016. *Kate Chopin: The Complete Novels and Stories*. Book House Publishing. Kindle Edition.

Douglass, Frederick. 2006. *Narrative of the Life of Frederick Douglass, an American Slave*. Urbana, Illinois: Project Gutenberg. Retrieved November 28, 2017, from www.gutenberg.org/ebooks/23. Kindle Edition.

Ellis, Havelock. 2005. *Little Essays of Love and Virtue*. Urbana, Illinois: Project Gutenberg. Retrieved November 21, 2017, from www.gutenberg.org/ebooks/15687. Kindle Edition.

Emerson, Ralph Waldo. 2012. *The Conduct of Life*. Urbana, Illinois: Project Gutenberg. Retrieved January 3, 2018, from www.gutenberg.org/ebooks/39827. Kindle Edition.

Encyclopædia Britannica. April 27, 2017. Havelock Ellis. Retrieved December 04, 2017 from https://www.britannica.com/biography/Havelock-Ellis.

Hanson, Erica. 1999. *The 1920s: A Cultural History of the United States through the decades*. Lucent Books: San Diego, California.

James, William. 1925. *Talks To Teachers On Psychology; And To Students On Some Of Life's Ideals*. New York: Henry Holt and Company. Kindle Edition.

Keller, Helen. 2000. *Story of My Life*. Urbana, Illinois: Project Gutenberg. Retrieved November 17, 2017, from www.gutenberg.org/ebooks/2397. Kindle Edition.

Levine, Richard A. 1967. *Backgrounds to Victorian Literature*. San Francisco: Chandler Publications.

Lubbock, Sir John. 2005. *The Pleasures of Life*. Urbana, Illinois: Project Gutenberg. Retrieved January 3, 2018, from www.gutenberg.org/ebooks/7952. Kindle Edition.

Mais, S. P. B. *Why we should read*. Urbana, Illinois: Project Gutenberg. Retrieved November 16, 2017, from www.gutenberg.org/ebooks/3015. Kindle Edition.

Mansfield, Katherine. 2007. *The Collected Stories of Katherine Mansfield*. Penguin Books. Kindle Edition.

Schreiner, Olive. 2008. *The Story of an African Farm*. Urbana, Illinois: Project Gutenberg. Retrieved December 1, 2017, from www.gutenberg.org/ebooks/1441. Kindle Edition.

Stalcup, Brenda. 2002. *The Industrial Revolution*. San Diego: Greenhaven Press.

Twain, Mark. 2009. *What Is Man? and Other Essays*. Urbana, Illinois: Project Gutenberg. Retrieved February 8, 2018, from www.gutenberg.org/ebooks/70. Kindle Edition.

Wilbur F. Gordy. 2011. *American Leaders and Heroes: A preliminary text-book in United States History*. Urbana, Illinois: Project Gutenberg. Retrieved November 21, 2017, from www.gutenberg.org/ebooks/35742. Kindle Edition.

Wilde, Oscar. 2008. *The Picture of Dorian Gray*. Urbana, Illinois: Project Gutenberg. Retrieved November 16, 2017, from www.gutenberg.org/ebooks/26740. Kindle Edition.

CHAPTER 2 REFERENCES

Anderson, Sherwood. 2004. *Triumph of the Egg and Other Stories.* Urbana, Illinois: Project Gutenberg. Retrieved April 17, 2017, from www.gutenberg.org/ebooks/7048. Kindle Edition.

Aristotle. 2005. *Ethics.* Urbana, Illinois: Project Gutenberg. Retrieved June 25, 2017, from www.gutenberg.org/ebooks/8438. Kindle Edition.

Baldwin, James Mark. The Story of the Mind. Urbana, Illinois: Project Gutenberg. Retrieved June 25, 2017, from www.gutenberg.org/ebooks/20522. Kindle Edition.

Benson, A.C. 2004. *The Training of Imagination* in *Cambridge Essays on Education.* Urbana, Illinois: Project Gutenberg. Retrieved January 8, 2018, from www.gutenberg.org/ebooks/13548. Kindle Edition.

Bloom, Harold. 2003. *Sherwood Anderson.* Chelsea House: Philadelphia

Chesterton, G.K. 2008. *What I saw in America.* Urbana, Illinois: Project Gutenberg. Retrieved November 25, 2017, from www.gutenberg.org/ebooks/27250. Kindle Edition.

Dewey, John. 2009. *The Child and the Curriculum.* The University of Chicago Press: Chicago. Retrieved April 7, 2017, from www.gutenberg.org/ebooks/29259. Kindle Edition.

Dewey, John. 2011. *How We Think.* Urbana, Illinois: Project Gutenberg. Retrieved November 27, 2017, from www.gutenberg.org/ebooks/37423. Kindle Edition.

Dewey, John. 2012. *Human Nature and Conduct: An introduction to social psychology.* Urbana, Illinois: Project Gutenberg. Retrieved October 16, 2017, from www.gutenberg.org/ebooks/41386. Kindle Edition.

Dictionary.com Unabridged. Random House, Inc. Dec. 2017.

Douglass, Frederick. 2006. *Narrative of the Life of Frederick Douglass, an American Slave.* Urbana, Illinois: Project Gutenberg. Retrieved November 28, 2017, from www.gutenberg.org/ebooks/23. Kindle Edition.

Eliot, George. 2006. *Adam Bede.* Urbana, Illinois: Project Gutenberg. Retrieved November 5, 2017, from www.gutenberg.org/ebooks/507. Kindle Edition.

Greg, William R. 1877. *Life at High Pressure* in *Literary and Social Judgments.* Vol II. London: Trübner & Co., Ludgate Hill.

James, William. 1890. *Habit.* H. Holt and company. Retrieved October 15, 2017 from https://archive.org/details/habit00jamegoog. Kindle Edition.

James, William. 1925. *Talks To Teachers On Psychology; And To Students On Some Of Life's Ideals.* New York: Henry Holt and Company. Kindle Edition.

Kinneavy, James L. and Warriner, John E. 1998. *Elements of writing.* Holt, Rinehart and Winston: Harcourt Brace & Co.

Leadbeater, Charles. 2016. *Nobody Is Home.* Retrieved November 27, 2017, from https://aeon.co/essays/why-theres-no-place-like-home-for-anyone-any-more.

Lubbock, Sir John. 2005. *The Pleasures of Life.* Urbana, Illinois: Project Gutenberg. Retrieved January 3, 2018, from www.gutenberg.org/ebooks/7952. Kindle Edition.

Stalcup, Brenda. 2002. *The Industrial Revolution.* San Diego: Greenhaven Press.

The American Heritage® Dictionary of Idioms by Christine Ammer. Houghton Mifflin Company. Dec. 2017.

Toohey, Peter. 2011. *Boredom: A Lively History.* Yale University Press. Kindle Edition.

Benson, Arthur Christopher. 2004. *Cambridge Essays on Education.* Urbana, Illinois: Project Gutenberg. Retrieved November 26, 2017, from www.gutenberg.org/ebooks/13548. Kindle Edition.

Wilbur F. Gordy. 2011. *American Leaders and Heroes: A preliminary text-book in United States History.* Urbana, Illinois: Project Gutenberg. Retrieved October 29, 2017, from www.gutenberg.org/ebooks/35742. Kindle Edition.

CHAPTER 3 REFERENCES

Brontë, Charlotte. 2007. *Jane Eyre: An Autobiography*. Urbana, Illinois: Project Gutenberg. Retrieved November 16, 2017, from www.gutenberg.org/ebooks/1260. Kindle Edition.

Butler, Samuel. 2007. *Essays on Life, Art and Science*. Urbana, Illinois: Project Gutenberg. Retrieved January 5, 2018, from www.gutenberg.org/ebooks/3461. Kindle Edition.

Chesterton, G.K. 1912. *Charles, Dickens, The Last of the Great Men*. New York: The Press of the Reader Club.

Chesterton, G.K. 2007. *Appreciations and Criticisms of the Works of Charles Dickens*. Urbana, Illinois: Project Gutenberg. Retrieved December 28, 2017, from www.gutenberg.org/ebooks/22362. Kindle Edition.

Chopin, Kate. 2006. *The Awakening and Selected Short Stories*. Urbana, Illinois: Project Gutenberg. Retrieved January 28, 2018, from www.gutenberg.org/ebooks/160. Kindle Edition.

Crystal, David. 1996. *English: The Global Language*. Washington, D.C. U.S. ENGLISH Foundation.

Dickens, Charles. 2008. *Oliver Twist*. Urbana, Illinois: Project Gutenberg. Retrieved November 4, 2017, from www.gutenberg.org/ebooks/730. Kindle Edition.

Eliot, George. 2006. *Adam Bede*. Urbana, Illinois: Project Gutenberg. Retrieved November 5, 2017, from www.gutenberg.org/ebooks/507. Kindle Edition.

Emerson, Ralph Waldo. 2005. *Essays*. Urbana, Illinois: Project Gutenberg. Retrieved January 25, 2018, from www.gutenberg.org/ebooks/16643. Kindle Edition.

Greg, William R. 1877. *Life at High Pressure* in *Literary and Social Judgments*. Vol II. London: Trübner & Co., Ludgate Hill.

Hughes, Kathryn. 2014. *The figure of the governess*. Retrieved December 29, 2017 from https://www.bl.uk/romantics-and-victorians/articles/the-figure-of-the-governess.

James, Henry. 2006. *The Bostonians, Vol. I (of II)*. Urbana, Illinois: Project Gutenberg. Retrieved January 9, 2018, from www.gutenberg.org/ebooks/19717. Kindle Edition.

Myers, D., Abell, J., & Sani, F. 2014. *Social psychology*. London: McGraw-Hill.

Priestly, J.B. 1992. *An Inspector Calls*. Pearson Education Limited.

Russell, Bertrand. 1935. *In Praise of Idleness and other essays*. George Allen & Unwind LTD: London

Schreiner, Olive. 2008. *The Story of an African Farm*. Urbana, Illinois: Project Gutenberg. Retrieved December 1, 2017, from www.gutenberg.org/ebooks/1441. Kindle Edition.

Various. 2004. *Cambridge Essays on Education*. Urbana, Illinois: Project Gutenberg. Retrieved November 26, 2017, from www.gutenberg.org/ebooks/13548. Kindle Edition.

Wollstonecraft, Mary. 2002. *A Vindication of the Rights of Woman*. Urbana, Illinois: Project Gutenberg. Retrieved January 9, 2018, from www.gutenberg.org/ebooks/3420. Kindle Edition.

www.ingramcontent.com/pod-product-compliance
Lightning Source LLC
Chambersburg PA
CBHW080849010526
44115CB00015B/2775